D0560654

TO LOVE IS CHRIST

David Teems

TO LOVE IS CHRIST

*The quoted ideas expressed in this book (but not scripture verses) are not, in all
cases, exact quotations, as some have been edited for clarity and brevity. In all cases,
the author has attempted to maintain the speaker's original intent. In some cases,
quoted material for this book was obtained from secondary sources, primarily print
media. While every effort was made to ensure the accuracy of these sources, the
accuracy cannot be guaranteed. For additions, deletions, corrections or clarifications
in future editions of this text, please contact Paul Shepherd, Senior Acquisitions
and Development Editor for Elm Hill Books.
Email: pshepherd@elmhillbooks.com*

Products from Elm Hill Books may be purchased in bulk for educational,
business, fundraising, or sales promotional use. For information, please email
SpecialMarkets@ThomasNelson.com

Scripture quotations are taken from:

New Century Version®. (NCV) Copyright © 1987, 1988, 1991
by Thomas Nelson, Inc. All rights reserved.

Scripture quotations marked (KJV) are taken from the Holy Bible,
King James Version, Cambridge, 1769.

Scripture quotations marked (NIV) are taken from The Holy Bible:
New International Version (NIV). Copyright © 1973, 1978, 1984 by the
International Bible Society. Used by permission of Zondervan Publishing
House. All rights reserved.

Scripture quotations marked (NKJV) are taken from The Holy Bible:
New King James Version (NKJV). Copyright © 1979, 1980, 1982 by
Thomas Nelson, Inc. Used by permission. All rights reserved.

Scripture quotations marked (ASV) are taken from the New American
Standard Bible®, Copyright © 1960, 1962, 1963, 1971, 1972, 1973, 1975,
1977, 1995 by The Lockman Foundation. Used by permission.

ISBN: 1-4041-8554-2 *(hardcover)*

Project Manager: Alice Sullivan   Design: Margaret Pesek

Who chooseth me must give and hazard all he hath.

—*William Shakespeare*

The seams of this little book bulge with life, life that acts like life, and with love that behaves like love, with all its unpredictability, with all its healing qualities, all its warm mystery, at least as much as can be assigned to language. And these pages are browser friendly. Skip around if you want. There's no order to it anyway. Some things will not be confined to a sequence, to a procession of days, to our need for order, or to reason itself. Love is one of them. It's charged with way too much divinity. It hums with too much hidden life. But I'm giving too much away. Here's a secret: *This is a book of love. It only thinks it's a devotional.*

David Teems

For J.D.

JANUARY

Christ, where forever keeps itself in me

THE BOOK OF LOVE

Beautiful words fill my mind. I am speaking of royal things.
My tongue is like the pen of a skilled writer.—Psalms 45:1 NCV

You, reader, are love's truest book in a world starving for divine
literacy. A good read by any light, you are the gospel they seek.
Love with hands and eyes, that which books and creeds cannot
give. Even books like this one you hold in your hand are but
mimics, for *only life can give back life.* Text has little commerce
with the soul. Perhaps this is why Jesus wrote nothing at all,
except in the dust and in the warm living chronicles of the
human heart. *So let them turn back the leaves! Let love wake where
it sleeps! Clear your throat of mortality and let the deep springs groan!
Let the pipes rattle and the foundation shake! Let divinity and
innocence, sincerity and warmth gather sweet again in the mouths
of lovers and holy men, handmaidens, and all you sons of thunder!*

**In Christ, Who gave the ink of love its crimson,
the rose of love its blush, Amen**

May heaven never stop writing its testament of love within you.
The book of love has the strangest of literary qualities, that of
being continually written and long finished at the same time.

January 2

All of God lives in Christ fully. —Colossians 2:9 NCV

God is love. —1 John 4:16 NIV

To define Christ, to catalogue, or to sort out the elements that gave Jesus his Christness, is to get as close to a definition of love as we may get. In those elements, we have all the proofs we need, all the conditions necessary to recognize love in a world of counterfeits, a world of imposture and pretended images. *Surrender, sacrifice, humility, kindness, devotion, faithfulness, truth, selflessness, intimacy, otherness, mystery, as well as a warm mix of divinity and humanity that puts the stuff of Forever in love. Love itself is an incorporation of all these conditions, as well as the inexpressible, the undefinable, things that defy our lists.* How am I to know true love? How am I to recognize it when it comes? How am I to recognize it in myself and the shape it takes in me? I need look no further than its blueprint, no further than…

Christ, where life and love mingle as in a common cup, Amen

To love is Christ. May He be the template by which love shapes itself in you.

JANUARY 3

For our citizenship is in heaven...—Philippians 3:20 NKJV

I am bred of heaven. And though earth grows more distant in me, I am meet for the worlds you have appointed for me today. Show Your kindness through me. Write welcome upon my face. Set invitation adrift in the tides of my blood. Fan the deep ovens of my faith to flames till I am warm to the touch, right for feasting in a world of famine.

In Christ, *food of life, Amen*

May love give you access to the higher instincts within you, those we share with divinity, that we may have lost in our distractions or in our attempts to explain.

JANUARY 4

Behold, I have received a command to bless...
  —Numbers 23:20 NKJV

Each page in this book closes with a benediction. I just thought I'd explain.

It's what love does to the speech. Benediction may be defined as blessedness on assignment, a warm outwardness, benevolence in verbal packing, blessedness that is extroverted, generous, and unreserved, love in transit, love in audible currency, tendered in little pithy bursts of goodspeak, like little gospels that unfold in a celebration of promise and possibility. A benediction resonates joyful on the tongue like a poem or a proverb and there is nothing finer, there is perhaps no higher music, no more sacred art, than blessedness when it is found in the mouth of sincerity. *It's evidence of indwelling deity, the voice of the inner temple asserting itself in the liturgy of life. All you really need is blessedness and a mouth to put it in. Love will do the rest.*

In Christ, *the Word forming in my mouth, Christ, this audible feast, Christ, at the close of all our pages,* **Amen**

May all that has been reduced to noise in you become music again.

RIOT AND OVERTHROW

When they came to Jesus, they found the man sitting at Jesus' feet, clothed and in his right mind, because the demons were gone. But the people were frightened.—Luke 8:35 NCV

You expected something else perhaps, but it was riot and overthrow, no less than anarchy, a change of government, a dispossession, a divestment of rule. For Self is deposed, dethroned at last, as well as the many myths that sustained it. All things have changed and out there before you is the world you only thought you knew. *Love shapes you by its own template, by its own wonderful idea of you.* And it gives you no options. Love is the stuff that gives back divinity to life, that makes life the adventure God intended it to be.

**In Christ, the shape love seeks in me,
heaven's idea of who I am, Amen**

May love awaken the explorer in you, the pioneer, the inventor, the holy man, the adventurer. May you find in you the stuff of Mr. Rogers and Indiana Jones, of Mother Teresa and Captain Kirk, all within the same bustling living space that you occupy.

ADAM'S PRAYER

JANUARY 6

The love that moves the sun and other stars.
  —Dante Alighieri (1265-1321) *Divine Comedy: Paradiso*

Lord, though I am the first, many will come after me, multitudes like myself who will search the earth for home again, who will find only in love what they seek to still their hunger. When love awakens in them, they will no less feel what I felt when I saw the first daybreak, when I felt the grass of Eden beneath my feet, and spoke with You as a friend in the cool of day. Ages will pass and quickly, but love is the same, now, in me, as it will be for those who read this, those lovers distant and unborn, those echoes of You, those shining stars, those reflective moons. Love is. Love was. Love is yet and always to come. It will remain long after time erases the stray marks from this page.

In Christ, our first daybreak, when love wakes at last, Amen

If someone asks "Who are you?" may you say, *"I am life in process. I am largeness finding itself. I am a work in progress. I am no less a gospel, a love letter written by the sure hand of Majesty, crafted in a secret place where the Good Author toils in sweetness. I am a poem forming in the mouth of God, a psalm ascending, an ecstasy rising in the midst of all my disenchantments. I am contentment in the heart of deity. I am awake."*

An Irresistible Drift

Follow the way of love… —1 Corinthians 14:1 NIV

"Follow me."—Jesus in all the Gospels

There is a momentum the heart will follow when it finds it, an impulse, an irresistible drift, a current upon which it may yield and free itself, a stream that runs in a single direction, a cadence by which we may know our true step, a tide that may cradle and carry us, a propensity that is soul specific, that has your name and His seal upon it, by a script written in a careful hand. It tells us who we are in a world of phantoms. It gives us singularity and selfhood in a world of masked men. And it's along this path we find the little evidences of our homeland, that thing that haunts the soul.

In Christ, the Lord of tides and all deep running streams, Amen

May your soul be large and boundless, wine dark and oceans deep.

JANUARY 8

The LORD will write in the register of the peoples: "This one was born in Zion." As they make music they will sing, "All my fountains are in you."—Psalms 87:6-7 NIV

In a day of solitude, may love be your host among the quiet hours. In a day of action, may love be the sweetness in your labor, your strength, your standard, your conspicuous garment, your provision, your reserve. In a day of challenge, may love be your strong underpinning, your immovable conviction that outweighs and outlasts all opposing strengths. In a day of retreat, may love be your regathering place, your place to come inside. In an arid season, when the soul aches with dryness, may love lead you to her hidden springs. Zion means 'parched place.' May you come to love the riddle of her name. And may you never lack the thing you truly need. *Life is thirst. Love is water.*

In Christ, *my craving, my contentment, all I ask of life,* **Amen**

May Christ have all access, all rights to you. May you drink from the cup He gives you. May it be your deep joy, the thing you can't explain about your tears.

WHEN IT REIGNS

"For indeed, the kingdom of God is within you."
—Luke 17:21 NKJV

My soul is vast, a realm in itself, fitted for all the shapes and dimensions of Highness, for royal habitation and all the endowments of Majesty. Take Your rightful seat, Lord. I know what I ask, for love is a living thing and life doesn't begin without pain. Grind me as wheat if You desire bread, for it is I who hunger. Crush me and hide me away if Your thirst is deep enough, for my throat aches with dryness. Mint me into coin. Spend me at Your pleasure, O God, for my purse is hollow and threadbare. Loose Yourself in me. Come over me like a flood tide. Love is a graceful monarch. When it reigns, it pours.

In Christ, this prayer laboring in me,
Love on assignment, Amen

May He Who is the God of heaven impose that same heaven upon you, making His conquest of your vast inner kingdom complete, the dim otherland, this life inside you that has sight and thought, but has known no rule, no god but you.

January 10

He who does not love does not know God, for God is love.
  —1 John 4:8 NKJV

Mystery unsettles us, especially in a day when knowledge is imperial and Self has become the common religion of the age. And yet knowledge, as exalted as it is, as venerated as it is in the high church of the mind, is a nonissue, irrelevant when weighed against the *'knowledge of God'* which has little to do with learning and has everything to do with love. He will not be found in nor understood by our best science or even our best theologies. He's too cunning, too elusive, too evasive for our traps, His ways too high. *Faith knows where to find Him and by what name He is known. The heart alone knows where the maps are kept.*

In Christ, love with a name we may speak, Amen

May you embrace the mystery of God, celebrate His living, teeming, and lovely Unknown. For the only certainty we may boast is this great and divine uncertainty.

I want them to be strengthened and joined together with love so that they may be rich in their understanding. This leads to their knowing fully God's secret, that is, Christ himself. In him all the treasures of wisdom and knowledge are safely kept.—Colossians 2:2-3 NCV

Lord, we feel we must unravel all mysteries, reduce the unknown to things we can see and measure, things we can have dominion over, for riddles are for children and storytellers. And so the world gets smaller, even as the number of secrets it keeps. But Love will not be gathered in our nets, by the cunning of our traps. Within me there is a bright and lovely innerworld, the seat where love sits, the Christ-place, where God is enthroned, where heaven and earth meet and agree together, an elevated place, higher than reason, deeper and more telling than art, where intellect is passive and submits to a thing it cannot explain. You are the Lovely Unknown, the invisible God, in love so clear to me.

In Christ, my soul dark with mystery, lovely with light, Amen

May you find no more comfort in your illusions. May your household myths lose their place of residence.

JANUARY 12

And the Word became flesh and dwelt among us, and we beheld His glory, the glory as of the only begotten of the Father, full of grace and truth.—John 1:14 NKJV

Some things are just too good to be true. *But then, some things are too good and happen to be true.* Christ is one of them. In Him the earth had a God willing to tell us more about Himself, to give us a better look, to let us get close enough to touch Him, warm-blooded God Who willingly took on all the peculiarities of flesh, all the natural vexations you and I are programmed with, a God Who lived in the warm thickets of us, in the sweaty palm of us, Who was like us, no higher, no lower, just one of us. And as if that was not difficult enough to believe, when Heaven and Earth demanded a reckoning between them, He called the fury down upon Himself. He opened up a door that had been closed to me and called me brother. *No, I couldn't have made all this up. I didn't have to. It's so good, I may have tried. But I suppose I was saved from that too.*

In Christ, our warm-blooded God, Amen

When heaven seems aloof or distant and proofs are hard to come by, may love be all the evidence you need.

*Your word I have hidden in my heart, that I might not sin
against You!—Psalms 119:11 NKJV*

*Your Word, Lord, is set within my soul like a living inscription, like
notes upon a score, like an imprinted code, an undiscovered DNA,
indelible and irrepressible in my blood. It lives in me like music, like
deep poetry, the lyric of life eager to proclaim itself and show its
beauty to an unsuspecting world. O God, open my senses, liberate all
vents of mediation between You and me. Give me an appreciation for
the littleness of life. Give me the heart of an explorer, an adventurer,
that I may see Your fullness even within the smallest or most hidden
of worlds, in the tiniest of details. Your Word is my map even as it is
the light I read it by.*

Expecting, Amen

May the highest and the best within you suffer no restraint,
no impediments, no walls, no government but Christ. May
something in this very day awaken the giant in you, free
the champion, the large bounding humanity in you, with
divinity enough to set it apart, to elevate it.

Love Is a Lot of Things,
But Blind Ain't One of Them

JANUARY 14

He who loves his brother abides in the light…—1 John 2:10 NKJV

In spite of what the poets say, love is not blind, any more
than God is without light. Love is what it is because it sees.
It misses nothing. Like God, love, too, is an author, a writer,
an artist who labors in detail: the smaller the better. We are
but sketches, being shaped into a finished work, each one a
love story, each one a good read. *O, that I may see as love sees,
all things in their true shapes, all life in its highest possibility. That
I may see what beauty there is in this soiled world. That my senses
would hunger as much for justice and right proportions of things.
Love, be my vision, my eyes, my light, till all things are clear, till
Christ be revealed.*

In Christ, my eyes, my light, my blindness, my sight, Amen

May you defer all decisions to the mind of love, trusting its
economy, its government, its vision of who you are, its wisdom
in spite of what you may think, in spite of what your senses
may suggest.

LOVE WITHOUT CEASING

By day the LORD directs his love, at night his song is with me—a prayer to the God of my life.—*Psalms 42:8 NIV*

Love is a prayer we make to God, a prayer we make out of life itself, an offering that returns to Him what was deposited in us at our awakening, when love first aroused us and called us by name. It is a trust given and exchanged, and given again, a warm living current that passes between heaven and earth, between time and timelessness. Distilled of His own essence and without the interventions of speech, love gently perfumes the hall of the Great King. *Pray beyond words. Love without ceasing.*

In Christ, *the lover's prayer, Amen*

May your heart know its own speech. The world may just think you're singing.

PRAISE: THE BEST PETITION

Praise God, who did not ignore my prayer or hold back his love from me.—Psalms 66:20 NCV

Praise is the best petition we can make without having to ask for anything.

In Christ, the reply given before any request was made, Amen

May petition be swallowed up in praise. And may praise itself be the medicine that soothes the lovesick heart.

LOVE IS ALL THE REASON
THAT YOU NEED

For this is the message that you heard from the beginning, that we should love one another. —1 John 3:11 NKJV

Love. It's why we're here. There are no other reasons. Love is the proof of higher life, the evidence of deity among us. It's the Christianity we were designed for. It's life and faith simplified, out of the nets. Love is what God had in mind when He called us each by name. It's what having a soul is all about. It's the divine liberated in each of us. It's the debt we owe—to God, to life around us, to ourselves. It's our fare homeward. It's the redemption of every moment we have. It's the sacredness of life. It's whatever made Christ go to the cross. It's life outside of self and it's self fully realized. It's life in elevation. It's our mutual heaven. It's a warm inner temple made by God and a voice within each of us that is not our own. It's our soul in government. And it's so much more!

In Christ, *the Christianity we were designed for, Amen*

May love be all the reason that you need.

WHERE GOD HIDES HIMSELF

JANUARY 18

In the beginning was the Word… —*John 1:1 NKJV*

Some say scripture is *literal,* that every word is exact in meaning, set in its proper and unquestioned place. Some say *metaphorical, allegorical, symbolic, or parabolic.* Perhaps the truth lay closer to the seams, the commas, the sheer connective tissue that bind these elements together, so that scripture can be said to be all of these and still remain consistent with itself, and faithful to the truth we seek within its margins. *Mystery is the paste that sticks them together, the place where God hides Himself.* The lover will understand. He thinks he's listening to music anyway.

In Christ, where God hides Himself, Amen

May the Gospel in you be so casual, so loving, so alive, so warm and palpable, so easy in you, so much your natural response to life, so evident, so filled with concord, so sweet with otherness, so joyfully fluent in you, that agreement seems to follow you about, happy in your service, so much that it must sing or be silent.

Thy kingdom come. Thy will be done on earth, as it is in heaven.
   —Matthew 6:10 KJV

Love is inevitable. More than tomorrow's sun. It's irrevocable.
More certain than the stars whose bright lamps will go out.
Love cannot be altered nor repealed. It cannot be called back,
for Christ said, "It is finished." It is the current that flows
beneath us, that sweeps us to our ends. It is the daybreak, the
bright and deathless morning to which the world itself is
tending. Love is the true evolution of man.

In Jesus, our inevitable Christ, our firm Heaven,
our fixed Star, Amen

May love be the noticeable difference you make today. May it
be the single living banner of your faith, that visible, audible,
irresistible, inevitable, higher expression of who you are.

JANUARY 20

Now there was leaning on Jesus' bosom one of His disciples, whom Jesus loved.—John 13:23 NKJV

Maybe he had the heart of a poet. Maybe he was a lover by nature, by some predisposition of his soul. Or maybe it was just some happy accident of divine insight and illumination that allowed John to understand so clearly who Jesus was and why He was here. But I suspect love had everything to do with it, for it was John who wrote, *"God is love[1],"* the great lyric that was entrusted to him, the one he would write for the rest of his life, that distilled into all his ink and action, and was written so clearly in him. Christ Himself was the Word, and John his trusted Wordwright, the poet-prophet who would untangle mystery for us and tell us what love would have us to hear of itself. The true Revelation John gave us was not the account of an old man from Patmos, but what he alone in the beauty of his youth saw in Christ, what the others just didn't seem to get. At first.

In Christ, the high church of John, the lover of lovers, Amen

May every expression of your life proclaim that GOD IS LOVE. May all that life returns to you say the same.

1 1 John 4:8, 4:16

LOVE IS NOT A NEGOTIATION

For this is the love of God, that we keep His commandments.
—1 John 5:3 NKJV

Love is not a negotiation. It is a surrender. An absolute surrender. As absolute as the God to Whom it is due. A total giving, an absolute submission of my absolute self. I entrust my soul to something I do not fully understand, to something larger than my one life. Surrender gives love its sinews. And there is no middle ground, no margin of compromise. Love is one thing and not another. Love is absolute and demands a response from me that is itself absolute. It demands from me an *always* or a *never*, a *Yes* or a *No*, and if there's such stuff in me, love will find it out. *Love is where forever keeps itself.*

In Christ, *where forever keeps itself in me,* **Amen**

May you trust Christ in discipline. May you trust Him in surrender—surrender weaned of all its former conditions. May you trust Him with your limits and beyond them, in that span where you are yet a mystery to yourself. May you trust Him in the excesses love will ask of you.

JANUARY 22

Intreat me not to leave thee or to return from following after thee: for whither thou goest, I will go… —Ruth 1:16 KJV

Like love, prayer is always intimate. And though the prayers in this book are now public, you, reader, by your presence, are a participant, though silent and unseen. Existing outside time and space, it's possible for you and I to share these intimate confines, to let our mutual silences labor together in the hearing of our common and yet most uncommon God. I realize this is a lot to consider, but the risk is worth it. And I am convinced that even if I reveal some awkward or ugly thing about myself on these pages, I can't lose, nor will shame get the advantage, for love has invited me into this place and has extended a hand as well to you. Whoever you may be.

In Christ, our private exchange, Amen

May blessedness follow you about without shyness: audible, legible, a good read when someone is curious enough to look into the book of your life.

What Was He Thinking?

Beloved, now we are children of God; and it has not yet been revealed what we shall be, but we know that when He is revealed, we shall be like Him, for we shall see Him as He is.—1 John 3:2 NKJV

In love, there comes a moment when we begin to suspect the emerging of a truer form of ourselves, a liberation from all counterfeits and all imitations, when we realize that love sees with the eye of an artist, as one who toils for perfection and detail. *For you were His first thought, His good idea put to the labor of creation, His deep intent come to life. You were the unrest in Him, for until His inmost desire brought forth the humanity nested within it, He did not rest. He toiled and took from the vast reserves of His soul all the beauty and divinity compressed within it and scattered it upon a new and unsuspecting universe. He busied Himself with preparation, even as a groom prepares His house for the day of visitation. You were His first and honored guest. Never despair of who you are. Love has a different idea of you altogether.*

**In Christ, when love freed itself, when the unquiet
in God was quiet again, Amen**

May the pilgrimage before you be plainly marked and well lit. In an unsure time, may love be lamp enough.

JANUARY 24

A Song of Ascents. Of David. Behold, how good and how pleasant it is for brethren to dwell together in unity!—Psalms 133:1 NKJV

If we could but give Christianity a chance to breathe free again as it did in its toddling days when men were wild for it, in our maiden days, when we had no name to call ourselves but one. O, for those days again, when we were faint with love, when heaven trembled with hunger and we were the sweet apple. Come, Lord. The door of my house is unlocked.

In Christ, my suspense—expectation almost wild in me, Amen

May your Christ be a warm one. May your Christianity be a door and not a wall.

THE GOLDEN TURNSTILE

For it pleased the Father that in Him all the fullness should dwell, and by Him to reconcile all things to Himself, by Him, whether things on earth or things in heaven, having made peace through the blood of His cross.—Colossians 1:19-20 NKJV

When someone is reconciled to the love within you, they are reconciled to the Christ at its center, to the God of its source. When they have access to one—just one heart where love is enthroned—they have access to the God seated there, to the joys and the rights of citizenship. Love is the best evangelist, heaven's first orator, the world conquering crusader.

In Christ, the invitation stirring in my blood, Amen

May love pulpit your little life and be the unquiet Billy Graham in you, with a call that's irresistible. May your life cry aloud with invitation. May your soul be like a golden turnstile, a little Ellis Island where pilgrims, outcasts, and wanderers may come and find a country of their own.

JANUARY 26

Because you are precious to me, because I give you honor and love you…—Isaiah 43:4 NCV

There are just no other reasons in the mind of God.

In Christ, just because, Amen

May heaven cradle your dream till it wakes.

How Much Work
Does it Take to Be You?

Now we see a dim reflection, as if we were looking into a mirror, but then we shall see clearly. Now I know only a part, but then I will know fully, as God has known me.—1 Corinthians 13:12 NCV

It once took way too much work to be me. In looking back on my youth and the search for myself, the many forms of *me* seem so diverse, contrasting, and at times, even contradictory, like separate personalities each contending for dominance. I was but a vague preperson. In time, all that was *not me* seemed to pass quietly away (as living things will do with age and lack of life support). To be *me* became less and less work. To be *me* was beginning to be more enjoyable and I have a strong suspicion that love had everything to do with it. *Love is a selflessness that defines self, that tells us who we are in a world of pretenders and counterfeits.* Only in love can we know who we really are, who this *self* is that we are known by, that we sought for so long, that haunts us, that is, till love.

In Christ, my true reflection, Amen

May Christ be the good filter that cleans and purifies you completely of all things that are not authentically and truly and remarkably 'you.'

No Greater Love: A Living Martyrdom

Greater love has no one than this, than to lay down one's life for his friends.—John 15:13 NKJV

O, for a Christianity that teaches selflessness, a living martyrdom, naked sweet in the eye of God, a Christianity that doesn't trivialize love because of its failures at it, or its misunderstanding of it, or for the sake of some loftier or more fashionable precept of the faith. O, that love would have its chance among us as one who bids for sovereignty, as one who seeks to rule among a headless people. O, for the Christianity of Christ. Cleanse me, Lord, of my inward politics, of partiality and preference, for love has none. Take from me the desire and craving that gives selfhood to me, particularly where love toils for life among us. Let me be no impediment to love. I am but a speck, a cipher, an animation of dust. Make me invisible, even as Yourself, O God, nameless as You are. Let me be lightness upon the wind that carries me, the Christ that lifts me to myself. O, that I may be counted among martyrs and all true lovers upon this earth. That I may be counted among such a happy lot.

In Christ, this happy martyrdom, this world dead to me, Christ, the all-beautiful, the other me, Amen

May you never fear the martyrdom love will ask of you.

A GOD WHO FORGETS

"I, even I, am He who blots out your transgressions for My own sake; And I will not remember your sins."—Isaiah 43:25 NKJV

Love does not count up wrongs that have been done.
—1 Corinthians 13:5 NCV

Because He loves me, God tolerates no barrier between He and I. And His desire to love me is so great, He made a law that He Himself could not break. He set legislation against His own omniscience. *He's allowed Himself to forget. My offence becomes lost in His forgetfulness.* Only time—linear, sequential time, record-keeping time—allows any of us to look back, to look forward, to forget, and to remember. Eternity frustrates this order of things and renders time a nonissue. One is but master of the other. *Love looks beyond the ugliness that I cannot forget. It can keep no such memories, for there is no time to put them in.*

In Christ, God's forgetfulness, Amen

May love redeem your lost hours and flights of days that seem black on the calendar behind you, things that seem irreparable, that stain the memory with something ugly and unwashed.

THE HIGH LIFE

JANUARY 30

"My lord, because of the vision my sorrows have overwhelmed me, and I have retained no strength. For how can this servant of my lord talk with you, my lord? As for me, no strength remains in me now, nor is any breath left in me."—Daniel 10:16-17 NKJV

Love elevates life, deifies it, sets life at its maximum pitch; life that is truly life, life lived upon a summit. It lifts us beyond ourselves and into a holy place. And great heights have a strange effect on our awareness. The world becomes smaller. All threatening things are diminished in the eye of love. It can dizzy the senses. At such an altitude, breathing is difficult, making it harder to speak. Words are few anyway, for there is little need of them. It's easy to become faint. But perhaps I'm not telling you anything new. These are things that lovers know.

In Christ, *life lived upon a summit,* **Amen**

May blessedness gather itself about you as if music were playing, as if your little life were set to a score, a background theme that elevates every parcel of your day, that puts sweetness and psalmody back into the general chorus of life.

To Love is Christ—A Prayer, an Ecstasy, a Benediction

May Christ be the cornerstone of this day's exchanges, the brave light by which you find your way, the open book and mirror of your love today, wherever and however love may show itself. May you not fear whatever surrender love asks of you. May you reflect Him from glory to glory and to glory again, Him, Who said we would do greater things, that we, being less than Him, would do the works of Him, loving as He loves and as He has commanded, that we, not being Him, would enjoy a share of His own glory, a bit of heaven even in the smallest of love's triumphal moments: the glory that follows humanity doing divine things. Christ, in a simple act of kindness. Christ, in the littlenesses of life. Christ, in the words you choose. Christ, in the tone of your voice. Christ, in your silence. Christ, in giving someone your time, in giving sweetly, unexpectedly, for no return other than love itself, and by a smile that says they are important, that this moment is important, that this moment is theirs and that you are but a happy part of it, that they are not alone, that the kingdom of God is closer than they would suspect—just as close as love is.

In Christ, all the Gospel, all the Amen, all the benediction necessary.

FEBRUARY

Christ, what we seek in each other
if the truth were known

PROOF OF LIFE

God is love. Those who live in love live in God, and God lives in them.—*1 John 4:16 NCV*

God is only as real to you as love is. Love is proof of divine life. And the earth is in need of this proof, lovers to walk upon it, to heal its deep fissures, to tend the great wound in its heart.

In Christ, when we needed further proof, Amen

May you be a bright candle in an unbright world.

February 2

Let no one seek his own, but each one the other's well-being.
—1 Corinthians 10:24 NKJV

No, it's not a small borough in Scotland and you won't find any maps to get you there except for those written in the heart. Still, we are called by a sacred command to *Otherness*, an elevated form of selflessness, where love is disguised in the shape of my neighbor, who is my *other* self, that warm humanity outside me—as complex, as awkward, as shy, and as needful as I am. If I deny them love, I deny them Christ and I hoard something sacred from myself as well. Perhaps we do not know how linked we are in the great mystery of Him, how intimately we are joined with the *other* in such a way that all things which set me apart, which give me selfhood and determine who I am, act not in a solitude but in congress with all life about it. *Otherness,* not a bad place to live at all.

In Christ, the road to Otherness, Amen

May you discover life at its inner courts, the life that exists beneath the polish of our surfaces, where the brave and hungry meet.

My soul thirsts for You; my flesh longs for You in a dry and thirsty land where there is no water.—Psalms 63:1 NKJV

If the secrets of our hearts were known, I believe each of us wants nothing more than to engage with something, with someone, with some warm piece of humanity that we can't make vanish with our remote or silence at the click of an electronic rodent. Our magnets are too strong. The divinity within us is too restless, too denied. In the distances we keep and nurture between ourselves, in our lack of engagement, in keeping ourselves to ourselves, we deny the very milk that would sustain us. *Deeper still, love is how we commune in Him, how we partake of Him Who called this great flock into existence. I have access to the Shepherd Himself each time I love.*

**In Christ, what we seek in each other
if the truth were known, Amen**

May you never fear to give yourself freely and completely to another, with no thought of reward, to one whose secret heart is just as hungry for love and union as your own, whose humanity cries out just as loud, and just as deep.

FEBRUARY 4

"No man ever spoke like this Man!"—John 7:46 NKJV

You just can't say what John said (The Beloved or The Baptist) without poetry, without something akin to joy, a bit untamed, rummaging about the heart and igniting the deep warm center where it finds its speech. Peter, Paul, David, Job, Ruth, the prophets...*Christ made poets of them all*. All spoke with a barefooted majesty. It's also perhaps a slight mockery the way Jesus chose the twelve, defying a world of opinion, trusting the most exalted things to the lowborn, to the untutored, the baser metal of the earth, the common stock of humanity, these men who would change worlds and kingdoms. Love is fun that way. And so disturbing.

In Christ, this high music in me, Amen

May love teach you a better English and the sweet music of understatement.

LOVERS ARE LOSERS

For whoever desires to save his life will lose it, but whoever loses his life for My sake will save it.—*Luke 9:24 NKJV*

Under love's reign, possession, power, gain, ambition, celebrity, and all the common weights and encumbrances, as well as all your attachments to this world *lose* their charm and their authority in your life. Fear *loses* influence over you. It must rule in another world, finding no loyal subject in yours. Despair *loses* dominion over you, sorrow its dark beauty. Heaviness *loses* itself in thanksgiving. I think you get the idea. In love, we not only *lose,* but in celebration we begin to throw off, to jettison those properties and possessions that are incompatible with love, things for which love has no use.

In Christ, the sum of all that I have gained, Amen

May humility be the code that unlocks life when it seems secret and aloof.

A KISS OF LOVE

FEBRUARY 6

Greet one another with a holy kiss.—*Romans 16:16,*
  1 Corinthians 16:20, 2 Corinthians 13:12 NKJV

It was to be a standard, a law kept among us, a rule of engagement among ourselves. What changed? When did we reorder order? When did we begin to hoard our kisses and hold back the hand of fellowship? Let us be free again. Let us disarm mystery and suspicion between us. Let us dismantle our arguments. Let our countenance become warm and alive again with invitation, with love eager to engage, to impose itself upon us, to flourish upon our plots of humanity with concord and sweetness. That we may love as we did in the beginning of this bright new order, when we were desperate for each other, when God was pleased and easy among us, when love was the only code between us, when there were no secrets, nothing owned that wasn't shared. That even in an age that has lost its sense of touch, we may dare to set our hopes again upon the cheek of friendship.

In Christ, *heaven's first kiss, the one you always remember, Amen*

May your next embrace, your next handshake or hug, however casual, your next kiss, however tender or light, be no less than a prayer we make without words, weightless and warm.

Of Blood and Tenderness

And these things we write to you that your joy may be full.
—1 John 1:4 NKJV

Sadly, to many of us, love is a fiction. Nonetheless, it is based on a true story. Because of our many myths and misgivings about love, it is a story that takes faith to believe. It's complicated. There's deceit. Betrayal. There's blood. Injustice. Cruelty. Religious madness. There are voices from heaven, visions, wonderful and frightful things, the dead raised, donkeys that talk, great fish with a taste for the prophetic, and doves that come out of nowhere. A child born to a maiden and to a God. And war. Lots of war. Sex. Mistaken identity. Miracles and more blood. Men seeing for the first time. A people wandering the earth and finding their way back home at last. It is all these. And yet, most of all, it is a story of redemption, a mystery of blood and tenderness— Love working out the details.

In Jesus, the Christ of blood and tenderness, Amen

May love be conspicuous, outward, daring. May it be no less the riot, the storm of your undoing, from which there are no shelters.

If You Love Me

"If you love Me, keep My commandments."—John 14:15 NKJV

We are here to love, to live life in response to a single command, and yet a command so strong, so severe in the heart of God, He didn't trust us to figure it out on our own. Rather, He showed us how it was to be done, writing Himself into our own history and into a gospel as deathless as He. Against love so extreme, all other things that we spend ourselves on in this life fade to inconsequence. Love isn't easy, any more than God is. It's too jealous, it contends too strongly against the great illusions of this world. But it gives me back my full and original humanity. It's the first order of my faith. *It's the highest praise I have within me.*

In Christ, something deeper in all of us, Amen

May you give up your theology for love, your beliefs, your agenda, your opinions, your assessments, your judgments, all your encumbrances, all weights and impediments, all these for something better, higher, more enduring and divine. May you discover the Rumpelstiltskin hidden from your eyes. May you exchange all your straw for gold.

2   John 13:34

TREAD SOFT INTO THE HOUSE OF LOVE

Blessed are they that wash their robes, that they may have the right to come to the tree of life, and may enter in by the gates into the city.
—Revelation 22:14 ASV

Love is not a plaything…—John Keats (1795-1821)

Tread soft into the house of love. Even as you would enter the court of God, pass through the door of invitation with caution in your steps, accompanied by the twin hosts, humility and yielding. In other words, take love seriously. It deserves your best attention. *Lord, I have been bold when I should have been afraid. I have been afraid when there was no cause. You have opened the sealed door that I may enter freely into the house of love, whose reach spans heaven and earth, whose domain is boundless. Therefore, I will let caution rule my steps. I will keep a sleepless vigil in my soul. Let me miss no opportunity to love. O Sweet Alarm, I am wakeful and watching.*

In Christ, my wakefulness, Amen

May you mimic God in His consistency, in His singleness, in His changelessness and yet may you do this as you continue to grow and evolve, as you continue to amaze yourself, as you continue to embrace this lovely puzzle of life, to embrace your own mystery, as alive with divinity as the God who set it in place.

By The Braille of The Heart

Do not stir up nor awaken love until it pleases.
  —*Song of Solomon 2:7, 3:5, 8:4 NKJV*

Almost unnoticed, someone approached me. It was a girl I had
not seen before. She had a dark beauty that both arrested you
and set you at ease in the same moment. My heart didn't race
(much). Everything stayed in place. The light where we stood
was amber and easy. Perhaps if I had thought about it then, I
would have said it had a certain intimacy in it. I just remember
feeling pleasant and safe, especially when she spoke. Sincerity
seemed easy for her and her speech had all the familiarity and
casual custom of friendship in it. She was lovely and with a
loveliness that she alone would be the last to notice. No, more
than that. If I could have described angelic, it would have been
closer to what she was in these moments. Not just in features
but in something that could not hide beneath her surfaces, that
she allowed me to see. She came without veils and she was as
comfortable, as safe with me. By some higher instinct, by a thing
we could not explain, by some braille of the heart *we both knew.*
I'm sure I just described the first moment I met my wife.

In Christ, our mutual attraction, Amen

May love be warm to the touch like the heat of an altar fire.

FALLING IN LOVE

It is a terrible thing to fall into the hands of the living God.
—*Hebrews 10:31 NCV*

A leaf, a feather in the wind. When I began to understand the love of Christ, I began to rethink what it meant to *fall in love*, that odd and usually involuntary event of losing control, of being swept along by a power greater than ourselves, against which we have no defense, a thing that love does to the heart. We usually think of falling in love as it happens only in the initial stages of a romance, that comes in a shock of ecstatic electricity. But there is a falling that is a continuous event in the life of one who loves. It's called surrender. Love is not love without it. And it never ends. Our truest liberty is realized in giving over control, in yielding to that one power great enough to sweep us endlessly outward, otherward, heavenward, a continuing rapture that carries us beyond ourselves into a holy place. O, it is a dreadful thing indeed to fall into the hands of the living God, a wonderfully terrible thing, a breathtaking, life-reinterpreting thing. *And the higher the life, the sweeter the fall.*

In Christ, the greater fall of man, Amen

May you know safety within the cradle of His hands.

FEBRUARY 12

Our God comes, and he will not be silent. A fire burns in front of him, and a powerful storm surrounds him.—Psalms 50:3 NCV

You did not know what or who it was you were looking for. You did not know you were looking at all. You did not know that you were without her until she arrived. You did not know you were alone until the first sight of her. You did not know there was a breach, an unmended place within your soul. Until love. And suddenly there's no longer any order within your mind. Only anarchy. An unplanting of rooted things. Reason itself bends beneath the weight of love. Revolution and unrest stir within the vast tangle and tenements of the brain. For there is a change of government. Riot and overthrow at the toppling of a kingdom. And you didn't see it coming. Until love.

In Christ, my caution, my confidence, the great breach mended in me, Amen

May you discover new vistas, bright new heavens, vast and unimagined frontiers of yourself that you could not have dreamed.

THE BAREFOOT HUCK,
THE MISCHIEVOUS FINN

This is a great mystery…—Ephesians 5:32 NKJV
In you the rivers sing and my soul flees with them…—Pablo Neruda

I'm still amazed how a chunky little kid *(husky* was actually my word of choice in those days) growing up in Atlanta, of two parents and an older brother in a *Leave It To Beaver* world, and a little girl 500 miles above him on the map, like the True North she would become to him and would always be, growing up, doing little girl things, thinking little girl thoughts, dreaming little girl dreams, watching and mimicking two older sisters years ahead of her, how they could come together as husband and wife, how love could bring two souls together in perfect harmony, how two histories could be conjoined in a single kiss, how *me-ness* could give way to *we-ness,* by something inevitable, by some script already written in the heart, by a compass spinning silent and unnoticed that pilots the soul to its harbor, by all the little accidents of life that lead us. *And O, what medicine she is to me. The adventure and the enchantment never ends. I'm but the boy, the barefoot Huck, the mischievous Finn. Love is a river.*

In Christ, the big adventure, the current that carries me, Amen

May wonder and amazement never lose their influence over you. May love be your secret of sustained youth.

Note for the clueless: Tomorrow is Valentine's Day guys. Be alert!

Valentine's: A Rightly Sainted Day

February 14

Let the morning bring me word of your unfailing love, for I have put my trust in you. Show me the way I should go, for to you I lift up my soul.—Psalms 143:8 NIV

Now let love have its day! And let it last. Give it no sunset, no twilit sky, no dusk to hide itself away. Let every day be sainted in the calendar of your life, every day a Valentine, every day to celebrate love among us. Glorious. Mysterious. Imperial. Conspicuous. Incarnate God in our midst.

In Christ, my day in love, Amen

May the day itself celebrate you and your arrival to it. May you find sufficient height in your steps. May you find divinity in each stride, each action you take, each thought that labors in the brain, each word that the mind considers, each syllable that forms in the mouth, each movement no matter how small or unnoticed, how essential or how trivial, as if God were the motion that carried you along, that piloted your footsteps, that swept you heavenward even in the most common rites of the day.

LOVE AND THE MARKET PLACE

Love must be sincere.—Romans 12:9 NIV

Valentine items are now marked down 50% or less and the deflation will continue until the shelves are drained. *So much for love and the market place.* I laughed at myself, even if it was kind of a pitiful laugh, standing in line at the flower section of a local supermarket late in the day (yesterday, February 14) behind a long line of husbands, boyfriends, and others of the numb and clueless. Yes, we are the 'Guys.' But there's still poetry in the attempt. There's still romance in the drooping petals, beauty in the wilt and weary blooms. *At least that's what she lets me think.*

In Christ, what is beautiful about love, Amen

May romance be a way of life, a truer Christianity, ever warm with mystery and divinity, that filters into all things. May it fill your days with adoration, with hymns ever pressing themselves upon the heart, with devotion almost wild beneath your surfaces.

YES

The Son of God, Jesus Christ, that Silas and Timothy and I preached
to you, was not yes and no. In Christ it has always been yes.
  —*2 Corinthians 1:19 NCV*

It's love's first utterance. It's the High Priest of little words,
a courageous host in a world of the faithless and unsure.
It's the only accomplisher of great things in this life, the maker
of artists and holy men, of great achievers and of small ones.
Affirmation thrives in the heart of true greatness. As does our
capital word YES. So let it quicken in you. Let it rouse some
sleeping part of you that risks nothing, that dares nothing
beyond what is safe and guarded. Go on and take it, lay hold
of it, seize it, make this heroic little word your own. We won't
miss it. Love has enough YES to go around.

> **In Christ YEShua, love in the affirmative,**
> **the YES between you and God, Amen**

May you give your assent to God Who asks it of you, your
YES when it is required.

PARADISE

*"How awesome is this place! This is none other than the house
of God and this is the gate of heaven!"*—Genesis 28:17 NKJV

Love is paradise present, where God lives His life, heaven
gathered among us, Christ in the middlemost of us, love that
shelters you and I within a rich living foliage. *Lord, make me a
lover like Yourself, that I may be with You this day in paradise. Make
my life a heaven. O, what a revolution! What a new spin for a tilted
planet! Love would no longer be consigned to our songs or to dreams
alone, but would deify the smallest particulars of our lives. Heaven
would not be some obscure and distant place that we may only hope
for after death, but it would be ours even as You first prepared it.*

**In Christ, the gate, the very house itself, Christ,
Who clothes me in paradise, Christ, where God lives
His life in me, Amen**

May paradise be liberated in you. May it filter into every
parcel, every outpost of your little world, restoring its original
light, giving back something that was lost, and renewing a
lovely mysticism to life.

FEBRUARY 18

By this we know love, because He laid down His life for us. And we also ought to lay down our lives for the brethren.—1 John 3:16 NKJV

Love's martyrdom doesn't always spill blood, but my surrender must be that complete, that final. Love is a delivering up of self, allowing my own Judas his dark action against me. As God loved, so should I. And from one John 3:16 to the next, the message is clear: To love is Christ. *Just what did John hear as he laid his head upon the breast of Jesus at the table in eventide?*

In Christ, the beloved's beloved, Amen

May you be John-minded, John-warm, John-young, John-faithful, John-devoted, John-loving, and John-wise. May you summon smiles to the face of God at His first thought of you.

THE SHAPE MY WORDS TAKE
WHEN THEY SING

I also will answer my part, I too will declare my opinion. For I am full of words; the spirit within me compels me. Indeed my belly is like wine that has no vent; it is ready to burst like new wineskins. I will speak, that I may find relief; I must open my lips and answer.
—Job 32:17-20 NKJV

Lord, I labor to this end: that the lines, the subtleties, the contours, and gentle slopes of Your face would show themselves with each careful and considered stroke, with each stress and accent, in the music of each syllable, even among the shy and understated. That, by some higher English in me, love would have an articulation in this two minutes time. Till You come faithfully again, the truer poetry of these lines. Like a browser among lilies. As if desire in me had given You life.

In Christ, the shape my words take when they sing, Amen

Where love is owed, may your words be true and debt-satisfying tender. The more tender the better.

FEBRUARY 20

Love is as strong as death…—Song of Solomon 8:6 NCV

Christ liberated the divine within each of them. He set ablaze the flame of love in their hearts, kindled the very fire that put poetry in the mouths of the crude and unrefined. The twelve began to speak with the tongues of lovers and holy men. Death would eventually prove each of them (except perhaps John, who was a lover from the start, who understood the deep martyrdom of his surrender early on). Even so, as love became the warm center of their lives, death became a thing they thought little of. It was a nonissue. For they understood love's mastery over all things, the very GODness of love, the CHRISTness of the death that was appointed them. Love is what they lived for, what they willingly and happily died for. *And if the same is asked of you or me, take comfort in this: Love is not silenced by death. It's only sweetened by it.*

In Christ, life without barrier, love without hesitation, Amen

May you be fearless in the day of change, when love would ask another death of you, another inch of ground, another stretch of lonely road.

I WILL SHOW MYSELF TO THEM

"Those who know my commands and obey them are the ones who love me, and my Father will love those who love me. I will love them and will show myself to them."—John 14:21 NCV

In marriage, once the terms are contracted and sealed with a promise before God, the veil is removed. Innocence celebrates itself again. Intimacy quickens and flourishes. All is Eden. All is paradise. It will only cost you everything. And yet, in that moment, when surrender is complete, when you have put to death all options, love no longer will speak to you in parables, but plainly.

In Christ, my evident and unconcealed God, Amen

In love, may you know what it means to be the child and the adult, to be innocence and age at the same instant.

THIS IS LOVE

This is love, that we walk according to His commandments.
  —*2 John 1:6 NKJV*

You gotta love the guy! Who else dares tell us so plainly?
Who, with such audible fire and light, gives us something to
break the code in this riddle of life and faithfulness, who takes
the risk to say, *'this is love and nothing more'? O John, as lovely
in age as in youth, poet and chronicler of love, you who lived to be an
old man, whose aged eyes were brightened with revelation, with Jesus
uncurtained in visions of wonder, apocalypse, and timeless majesty.
You, whose end is a secret known between you and your Beloved.
If I, too, could lay at the table of God, where the holy bread warms
upon the rough wood, where the wine sparkles in the cup, if I could
rest my head upon His breast and listen to the hidden music, and if
I could find my Sabbath there, what could heaven give to me that is
not already mine?*

In Christ, *heaven as told to me by John,* **Amen**

When your accounts are read at last, may the word BELOVED
come to His lips.

That Love May Live and Prosper:
An Ecstasy of The Faithful

But for you we are in danger of death all the time.
   —Psalms 44:22 NCV

O, what Christianity would be if we were so brave! If we but lived the martyr's life! If we could loose the grip of our mortality, of our holdings in this life for the sake of love, for the sake of otherness, for the sake of so rich a gospel! O, that we would gamble our existence for the smallest of acts, to count our life as nothing against the majesty found in a simple act of kindness—selfless, invisible, eternal, charitable, ennobling, and elevating. O, that if asked, we would willingly and without thought or pause take a bullet for love, suffer some outrage, swallow down some injustice, that love may live and prosper but one more day on this tilted and ever spinning, ever cooling planet.

In Christ, that love may live and prosper, Amen

May you be love's warmth in a frost-bitten world, love's champion when the damsel is tied to the tracks, when only a hero will do.

FEBRUARY 24

I go to prepare a place for you.—John 14:2 NKJV

Imagine a place where fear cannot exist, where there is nothing
to feed it, a place where fear is banished altogether, where
there is an impenetrable defense through which it cannot pass.
Imagine a place where there is nothing to make you afraid,
within or without, real or imagined, a place where fear and all
its fellow conspirators—judgment, unkindness, condemnation,
criticism, neglect, alienation—have no place. Now imagine
a place where Welcome is written on every wall, where it greets
you at every bend and turn, in every voice, written upon every
smile and upon little notes suspended on your refrigerator
doors, written in the quiet of your most private chamber,
a welcome that says, *"I'm glad you're here."* Imagine that!
Heaven and earth meeting together, where the only problem
that exists is knowing where one begins and the other ends.

*Believing love is such a place, **Amen***

May you enjoy Him Who is the Life of your little house, the
Good Tenant, Who has enfleshed Himself once again with
hopeful humanity.

And if I go and prepare a place for you, I will come again and receive you to Myself; that where I am, there you may be also.
—John 14:3 NKJV

Imagine a place where there are no locks upon the doors, inside or out. Imagine a place where large windows feed the rooms with light, upper and lower rooms, large and small rooms, grand rooms, and the lesser, insignificant ones, with a joyful light, an easy light, light that takes panic out of the day, that silences all alarm, that redeems us from our shadows. Imagine a place where you may live an unguarded life, a place where intimacy is the rule and not the exception to the rule. Where shame has no voice, bitterness no hiding place. Imagine a place where you may think without restraint to the very pulse, spark, and atom of your undiscovered thoughts, where kindness will be father to all your actions, sweetness the mother to all your words. Imagine a place where God would feel at home. Only love. *Imagine that!*

In Christ, my home, my place in this world, Amen

May Christ be the temple within your temple.

LOVE AND THE THINGS THAT ARE CALLED BY THE NAME OF LIFE

FEBRUARY 26

...I came to give life—life in all its fullness.—John 10:10 NCV

Love is not the incidental part of life, the happy accident, or just something else we do in the sweep and fury of all other things we call by the name of life. As divine things do, love permeates, infuses and invokes itself into things, particularly things warm and human, into our working life, our play life, our secret life. Love chooses to weave itself among them, a vital and living filament, working its way into all our chemistries and living compounds. Essence mingling with essence, humanity and divinity striving together, giving connective tissue and sinews to our resolve, purpose to our working life, depth and freedom to our play life, law and limits to our secret life.

In Christ, life and love in concord, laboring together, Amen

May you find the way that the soul delights in, the current to which every sinew of your strength, every gift and endowment given you, every stalled or kindled talent within you is yielding. May you find yourself in the journey. *And know this: the journey is in you already. May love illumine the maps.*

THE LAW OF SELECTION

But God has chosen the foolish things of the world to put to shame the wise, and God has chosen the weak things of the world to put to shame the things which are mighty; and the base things of the world and the things which are despised God has chosen...
   —*1 Corinthians 1:27-28 NKJV*

I am chosen. By some decision, by some determination, some conclusion long settled in Your heart. And yet I know myself too well. I know too well the blind, wounded, and unkind thing concealed within me. Still, You love me. And You know more than I. O, Unreasonable Love. You sought me out, in a desert place, dry and lifeless. In my flight You pursued me. I did not choose You. I chose, rather, my own exile. Still, and without condition or restraint, You love me. And though I do not understand, though I strive for words and have none, give me light and sense, that I may collapse under my weariness and in this present sweetness rest in love's beautiful and unerring choice.

In Christ, the law of selection, my unreasonable God, Amen

May love remove all the dark sediments in your soul, all the smoke from the mirror.

LOVE: A MYSTERY
THAT EXPLAINS ITSELF

FEBRUARY 28

...that they may know the mystery of God, even Christ...
—*Colossians 2:2 ASV*

Love is a mystery that we may live out. Like God, love is its own explanation, the riddle and its answer. Love gives no tongue to explain itself anymore than God, and yet we can enjoy Him and live in Him and find our sufficiency, our completeness in Him. Like love itself, He is His own reward. He is His own explanation. There are things for which knowing does not apply. Love is one of them. It is a mystery and yet one that explains as much as it hides. I love this!

In Christ, this great riddle explained, Amen

May the word 'mystery' fade in your vocabulary. May it be absorbed in presence, in habitation, in demonstration, in submission, in the living essence of love as it filters into all your extremes and into all the small particulars of your life. May it become a word little thought of.

FEBRUARY 29

He determines the number of the stars and calls them each by name.
  —Psalms 147:4 NIV

Thunder, earthquake, wind, and fire. In our beginnings, You showed Yourself in wonders, a parent to our child. When we had no way to explain, we looked to creation itself for some expression that brought You closer to us. When it rained we could say heaven wept. When the mountain smoked and scorched the sky with flames, we trembled before You. But in the readiness of time, You came to us in a form that we did not recognize or suspect. We could not understand the descent of God any more than we could comprehend love disguised as one of us. And yet the mountain no longer smoked, the sky no longer wept. I was the fallen star, absent from Your sky and You could not rest till You set it back in place.

In Christ, Who calls them each by name, Amen

May you never doubt the goodness of God.

MARCH

Christ, when love needed a name
to call itself

IF THE WIND COULD BE HARNESSED

The wind blows where it wants to and you hear the sound of it, but you don't know where the wind comes from or where it is going.
—John 3:8 NCV

If the wind could be harnessed, if spirit could be reduced to names, to words, lists, catalogues, creeds or catechisms, if you could determine the weather or the shape of a cloud in tomorrow's sky, you may at last be able to determine the way of love, to plot its course, to fix charts. But I suspect that's asking too much. Love doesn't entrust itself to us that way. We learn love by love, even as we know God. And that's a start.

In Jesus, the Christ Who calls the winds to account, Who scripts nature itself, Whose gospel is never quiet, **Amen**

May love return innocence to you, innocence that lives by a faith it little thinks of.

LOVE IS MINDLESS

MARCH 2

So love each other deeply with all your heart.—1 Peter 1:22 NCV

Don't think, love! Let the sleeping Eden in your blood awaken, that green world we knew before we toiled, before we busied ourselves in distraction, the Christianity that existed before Christ was born, when the heart was imperial and love was all it knew, when ecstasy had sense, when love was innocent and aloof and had no age. *Warmth and touch need no thought. Love is higher than that. Intimacy is mindless. And all of love's exchanges are intimate.* Love did not begin with the mind and does little commerce there. I cannot talk myself into love for love exists where there is no argument. I cannot think it from me for it will not obey. Love just doesn't mind well at all. Anyway, love is charged with way too much divinity. It's too alive with mystery, guilty of too much unreason. Any of these sends the mind into overwhelm. And that's just too much to think about.

**In Christ, *where heart and mind agree and
live like friends, Amen***

May love give you understanding outside of what you see, what you think, and what you feel.

DO YOU LOVE ME?
QUITE JESUS OF YOU TO ASK

"Do you love Me?"—John 21:17 NKJV

Christ stripped Peter of his confidence, of his claims, his honor, his safety, all in one swift and unrelenting act of love disguised as death. When Jesus died, so did Peter's god and all the remaining illusions and supporting fictions he had woven together in the privacy of his heart. Being thrown into grievous overwhelm, the Rock was now broken into bitter and unrecallable pieces. Yet, and as is so very Jesus of Him, and with just enough time for grief to do its clarifying work, Christ, after His resurrection, asked Peter, *"Do you love me?"* I suspect Peter 'got it' at that point. The question itself was the founding stone of things to come thereafter and of all things Jesus. The church Peter was to father into existence was to be built upon the divine masonry of those four simple words.

In Christ, my finishing, the end of my illusions, Amen

When love divests you of your own myths, when brokenness leaves all you believed in unreclaimable shards and splinters, when Jesus gently whispers in your ear at last, *"Do you love me?"* may your soul rejoice in its response and at its rebirth.

GOD IS ALL I KNOW OF LOVE

MARCH 4

The Son reflects the glory of God and shows exactly what God is like.
—Hebrews 1:3 NCV

To love is Christ. Every action love takes, Christ. Every word it speaks, Christ. The large humanity in my touch, Christ. The sacredness of life, Christ. Love's mastery of death and time, Christ. The private exchanges in my home, Christ. The softness in my voice, Christ. The casual embrace of friendship, Christ. The sovereignty in an act of kindness, Christ. Divinity in me alive and dispersing itself warm into the world, Christ. Christ showed us what love was, how it behaved, and against the hostility of a world that could not understand. Love is how He explained God. A portrait in blood. Inside parable, outside of words, He was love's book. *Love is all I know of Him. And to know Him is everything.*

In Christ, what I know of love, Amen

May you pursue love in all things. Though quiet at times, love is never absent, no more than God could vacate your life or be banished from it.

Was It Something I Said?
O, I Hope So! (Part One)

"To him who overcomes I will give to eat from the tree of life, which is in the midst of the Paradise of God."—Revelation 2:7 NKJV

O, for a Christianity more taken with love than it is with its own traditions and histories, a Christianity not interested in 'movements' or the spiritual fashions of the hour, a Christianity that puts no argument in its mouth, that does not spend itself on proofs, a Christianity that is bigger than its sermons, whose worship is found in the unnoticed acts of kindness, of tenderness and warmth removed from the common eye, with love so large it cannot be fitted into our buildings but must gather outside itself to breathe, a Christianity found at a neighbor's door or at a widow's lonely table, at the bed of the dying or infirm, or in the frayed seams and loosening knot between a husband and wife, love courageous enough to be a shield around a child and his innocence or a maiden and her purity, that would intercede between a young man and his hunger, between an old man and loneliness.

In Jesus, the Christ I seek in Christianity, Amen

May your Christianity be just another name for love.

Was It Something I Said? O, I Hope So! (Part Two)

March 6

*Yet I hold this against you: You have forsaken your first love. Rememb[
the height from which you have fallen!—Revelation 2:4-5 NIV*

*O, for a Christianity that would break loose, that would liberate
itself from its moorings, Christianity that would love larger than its
name, larger than its credos and cant, than its catechism and campson[
a Christianity more real, more living than its images and its rhetoric, [
Christianity of the tender and the selfless, of medicine men and marty[
whose music is deeper than its hymnals, warmer and more irresistible
than the heat of its pulpiteers. O, for a Christianity that would measu[
itself against one simple act of charity and not by its achievements or [
numbers, a Christianity that lived up to the One Who called it out o[
the world and then back again, the One Who fathered its first steps, th[
clothed her nakedness with love, warmth, and divinity, who emptied
Himself in her behalf and called her His own and by His own name.*

In Christ, life recalled and corrected, Amen

May love silence your arguments, your theologies, your need f[
proofs and apologies, purifying your Christianity of them at la[
May all life show itself sacred in return. May you begin to rea[
scripture as a lyric, the way lovers do, for it was their own kin[
who wrote it.

MERCY

But go and learn what this means: 'I desire mercy, not sacrifice.'
—*Matthew 9:13 NKJV*

Mercy, love's noblest gift. Mercy, where God imposes Himself on the world through us. Mercy, where humility and majesty mingle, where humanity and divinity become indiscernible from one another. Mercy, the part of God that saves.

In Christ, the part of God that is mine, Amen

May you be counted among the merciful, among the Father's good mirrors. May mercy show itself first in your own home, within your own circles, among those of your own likeness, with whom we traffic the most. May mercy show itself in your own mirror, in the judgments we make of ourselves. May mercy be the cornerstone of all outwardness, of all trade with warm humanity. May your judgment feed where mercy dwells. May it be the light by which you read and discern life around you. May it be overflowing, evident in your speech. May it have access to the hands and sovereignty over the tongue. May mercy return upon you in like and unsought measures. May it have first chair, first voice in the great counsel where the soul seeks its way in this world.

MARCH 8

…Be content with such things as you have. For He Himself has said, "I will never leave you nor forsake you."—Hebrews 13:5 NKJV

When I asked my wife to tell me the first thing that comes to her when she considers love, she responded with a single word, 'Safe.' In our years together, I've witnessed the emergence of a large soul, benevolent, generous, warm, surrendered, soft, and selfless. She finds good in all things great and common, an uncommon thing in a world that's faithless and unkind. She could have been a weaver in a fairy tale, or an alchemist, whose trade is changing lead into gold. How many times I've stood by and watched silently as little miracles took place. The miraculous is commonplace with her, though she's the last to notice. Her heart is contentment. Safety dwells there. I know. It's my home.

**In Jesus, thought to be the carpenter's son,
the maker of safe houses, Amen**

May love build your house. May it be warm and safe, a place of contentment, a place where the authentic in you is realized, a womb of higher life.

Purge me with hyssop, and I shall be clean; Wash me, and I shall be whiter than snow.—Psalms 51:7 NKJV

O Crown of Earth, Door of Heaven, Shining Star of Midnight and Morning, sweep over my earth with mercies sweet and overpowering! Tread upon this rude and loveless world with conqueror's feet! Let the ground tremble in wakefulness! Let the heavens thunder with approval! Let the skies weep with joy! Let the winds exult among the great trees, let them sing the Redeeming time! Lord give me the faith it takes to forgive, to allow pardon, mercy, and reconciliation to unbind my soul. Be ruled, my heart! Let love take its rightful seat of government in me! Forgive me my offences, Lord. And forgiven, let me live in that warm generous light of my latter nativity, for I am reborn in love. Let mercy awaken the poet in me, the king broken into words, the David after Your own heart.

In Christ, my faith to love, my strength to forgive, my pardon before I knew to ask, Amen

May any unforgiveness die in you. May it choke on its own excess, its own venom. May it be mute, lifeless. May it leave no traces, no glowing embers to rekindle itself.

Love is an Emptiness

March 10

The earth was empty and had no form. —Genesis 1:2 NCV

There was unrest in God, an unsatisfaction gathering in proportions unimagineable to you and I. Creation itself was but the mirror of His discontent. Love was more than motive, it was The Life itself mounting up within Him, the thing that stirred like chaos and unorder, massing its jealous heat to brightness and to speech. Love spoke at last and order was set in place. The very template that was Christ—the Word—was set like architecture upon a wild and unstructured universe. *Love is an emptiness, a holy and sublime unsatisfaction, an unrest that only Christ can calm, a storm which hears but His voice alone.*

In Christ, my emptiness, my soul set to order, God at peace in me, Amen

May you take something sacred from each day, even as you bring something sacred to it.

I See Differently.
The Light Has Changed.

*And since I could not see for the glory of that light, being led
by the hand of those who were with me, I came into Damascus.*
—*Acts 22:11 NKJV*

His eyes would no longer tell him the things they had always
told him, for they were under new management, even as his
heart. The illusions and myths that had so long ordered his
world were broken up, dispelled in the great light of Christ.
The kingdom within him had found its King at last. May you
have no less than a revelation of love today. Bright. Electric.
Radiant. Paul may have simply called it Daybreak, after
so long a night. May you have the kind of awakening that
changes all things, that transforms your world, of which you
may say, *"I see differently. The light has changed."*

**In Christ, love's sweet lamp, the light
by which I read all things, Amen**

May your faith simplify in love's clarifying light.

It Stole the Romance

March 12

What manner of man is this, that even the winds and the sea obey him!—Matthew 8:27 KJV

The electricity was gone and by evening a host of candles lit the room, a constellation that sparkled in our eyes. We began to see each other in the amber glow of a softer, sweeter light. My wife, Benita, and myself, Adam, my oldest, his wife Katie, Shad, my youngest, Savannah, the dog, and Sugar, the cat. All together, laughing, talking, remembering, purring. It was a day in pause, a suspension of what had come to be normal. Life was old again. It took control from us and gave back invention, simplicity, wonder. The power came back on briefly, later in the night. It was abrupt, rude and interfering. It stole the romance. Something seemed to scatter from us, bidding us return to the life of ticking things, to our little cells peopled with appliances and conveniences and other lifeless things. But I was warm with revelation and with something remembered in me.

In Love, something electric rediscovered between us, the power that never really left at all, Amen

May your life be interrupted. May heaven exchange it for something better, something you forgot.

GOD IS NOT A VERB

"I AM WHO I AM." This is my name forever.
—Exodus 3:14-15 NKJV

Somehow *THE GREAT 'I DO'* just wouldn't have the same
poetry that we've come to love about His name. God is *being*.
He is not *doing*. He is Jehovah, the 'existing one,' 'the one
who is,' sufficient in Himself. God is love and therefore love
is not a verb either. It too is *being*. Not to do, but to be. Love
exists within itself, independent of action. We are said to be
in love. Action is the fruit of being. Doing follows being.
Deep isn't it? *Give me true rest, O God, true cessation, true pause
of my busy heart. Let me feed and nourish my soul in You. Let the
quiet no longer unquiet me. And in the yielding, in the undoing, in
the letting go, I will know who I am. I will know the action I am
to take. For I am in love, unmistakably, outrageously, and
irrecoverably in love.*

In Christ, *the only action love knows to take,* **Amen**

In all things, may love be the wisdom by which you act. And
may action follow being. BE, first. DO, as it comes to you, as
love leads.

THE KEY TO LOVE

But he gave up his place with God and made himself nothing.
  —*Philippians 2:7 NCV*

There is a key to love. Love is not love without it. It will not give up its secrets or remove its veil without it. It is the most difficult thing that will ever be asked of us. It will cost all you have and for no promise of reward other than love itself. Love is serious like that. Most of us, if we could whisper in God's ear and ask, "O MASTER, WHAT IS THE SECRET OF LOVE?" And a voice were to answer and say, "SURRENDER," I think most of us would come again and ask, "Uh, O MASTER, IS THERE ANOTHER?" Surrender is the key to love and its afterlife. Try to remember where you put it.

In Christ, the death that is asked of me, Amen

May your deeper sense become deeper still, another fathom, another death inward, another surrender, by deliberate abandon, another pace closer to the unimaginable YOU that you thought was but something you dreamed.

MARCH 15

"But who do you say that I am?"—Mark 8:29 NKJV

How am I to follow that which I do not fully comprehend, that I am not able to 'get,' which all my devices cannot explain? Christ is complex enough. He is not easy. How am I to unriddle Him, to give sense to the mystery of Him, to this, the Alpha, the first of some new and unsettling order of things? Love seems too easy an answer and yet by some instinct that I cannot explain, I know it is the right one and it is all the explanation the soul needs.

In Jesus, the Christ of all my questions and the love that silences them, Amen

May love transcend all your best arguments, all the many assessments we make of life. May it outlast the gaze and gossip of all human courts and all contending streams.

LOVE AND GOING THROUGH THE MOTIONS

MARCH 16

And love means living the way God commanded us to live.
As you have heard from the beginning, his command is this:
Live a life of love.—2 John 1:6 NCV

What do you do on those unlovely, unloving days? What do you do
with those mischievous little feelings that overpower you, that mock
the heart, that circle about you like some big craning predator bird
thing? What do you do on those days, those grey, overcast, *I-want-to-
be-alone-don't-bother-me-love-is-too-much-work* days? You go back to
the Book! You go through the motions! You summon it up! You *do*
love. Whatever it takes. You know the fundamentals. You know
enough about how love operates, what it expects. So you follow,
one step, then another. You obey. You task your own will. You shut
down all other voices. You war with yourself if you must. Engage it.
Set love in motion, however small its pulse of life. And if we fail,
we've at least attempted to open a door, to let light bleed through
a seam. I suspect that in some unknown, unexpected moment, love
itself will assume control again.

In Christ, the light that bleeds through all my seams, Amen

When wind and rain and other ill tempered elements beat down
upon you, may Jesus be your peace, the God of storms, the hand
that rocks your soul to calmness again.

A DAY OF PATRICK

Therefore, if anyone is in Christ, he is a new creation; old things have passed away; behold, all things have become new.
—2 Corinthians 5:17 NKJV

Let us celebrate a day of Patrick, whose devotion flowed in his blood like youth and ecstasy, with psalmody and fire. Patrick, for whom Christ was the pulse that beat about his heart, the strong and steady cadence that gave the evangelist his voice, gave the poet his song, and gave Ireland its greenness. *"Christ with me, Christ before me, Christ behind me, Christ within me, Christ under me, Christ over me, Christ to the right of me, Christ to the left of me, Christ in lying down, Christ in sitting, Christ in rising up. Christ in the heart of all who may think of me! Christ in the mouth of all who may speak of me! Christ in every eye which may look on me! Christ in every ear which may hear me!*[3]*"*

In Christ, the world green again, the new day upon me, **Amen**

May love be a conqueror to all your settlements, all your unyielded parts.

---

3 *Excerpt from THE LORICA (shield) of St. Patrick – 5th Century*

MARCH 18

Now I know in part, but then I shall know just as I also am known.
  —*1 Corinthians 13:12 NKJV*

We answer to mortality. We eat. We breathe. We sleep. We play. We die. Our lives flow out from us in linear procession. We are answerable to time, our bodies to the slow declining years and plundering elements. Still, love enfleshed itself, wrapped itself in base humanity, gave itself a heart and sandaled feet, offered itself to us before we asked, before we knew we were without it, before we knew we were lost. It gave us a way that we may follow, that we may find ourselves and Him Who sought us, that we may live confidently in love and under its rule, be shaped and formed by it, broken and sculpted on its wheel. For life itself is but one brief and indeterminable catechism. Till love. Till fully Him.

In Christ, my catechism, my canon of life, Amen

May you discover new worlds, galaxies unseen, vast and uncharted innerworlds of humanity so warm and so close to you. May love show you all its hidden charts. May you be a new Columbus on these strange and beautiful waters.

O, How Beautiful a Thing

These people are not drunk, as you think; it is only nine o'clock in the morning!—Acts 2:15 NCV

Love is unreasonable. It is a living thing and relies on none but its own compass, its own charts, conforms to none but its own shapes, takes none but its own counsel, and is not obligated to explain itself to us by our accustomed reason. Love is a gathering of flames we cannot harness, that teach us how to dance. It is a tide that stands against tides. It maddens and exalts. It elevates and debases. It is flirtatious and it is shy. It's a risk and yet has divinity enough to take risk out of risk and make risk seem tame. *O, how beautiful a thing is love. How mysterious[4]. How utterly OTHER than us. It took no less than Christ to explain what it was.*

In Christ, the shape love took when we needed to know, Amen

May love start a happy riot in your soul, irrevocable, irrepressible, that overthrows all the old guards, that mocks your former limits, that gives a new tongue to what's inside you, that liberates ecstasy and other anarchies in the blood.

---

4 musterion–(GR) mystery; a derivative of mus which means 'to shut the mouth.'

COMPLETENESS: GOD IN US

MARCH 20

No one has ever seen God, but if we love each other, God lives in us, and his love is made perfect in us.—1 John 4:12 NCV

Completeness: Life reordered according to divine standards. God living comfortably with us, natural and unopposed, as one welcomed in His own house. Harmony that disperses itself into our immediate world, to life as it gathers about us. An agreement of heaven and earth within us, where the two come together as one, Christ in the middlemost of us. And to all this there is a condition, the dread and wonderful *if*. *If* we love. For *if* we do not, we do not know God because God is love, in spite of our arguments, our apologies, in spite of the High Church of our natural intelligence. If you dig deep enough in the dirt, in the primal causes, it is love, or the absence or mismanagement of it that gnaws at the hidden root. *Love is easy. We are the work.*

In Christ, my humanity complete, my possession and my pursuit, Amen

May bitterness find no nesting place within the heart. May you take away all your consent, all the permissions you gave to it. May it exhaust itself for lack of feeding.

My soul shall make her boast in the LORD: the humble shall hear thereof, and be glad.—Psalms 34:2 KJV

Is surrender in you strong enough to liberate your soul to its simplest form, its purest identity, as heaven first imagined it to be? Is selflessness in you strong enough to clarify who you are? Does your soul have the submissive sweet magnetism of a child, that invites, and invites, and invites again, whose gentle invocations wound the Father's heart with an ache that only love and innocence can inflict? Or is your soul a secret, a guarded, hoarded thing? Or maybe worse, is it camouflaged, hidden within the hollow frame of a life that risks nothing, that gives nothing away? Consider the soul never really silent. What does it tell the world it encounters? What questions does it ask of those around you? Does it enlarge? Does it diminish? Does it invite or does it deny? Does it magnify or does it reduce? What does it demand? What does it feed upon? What does it give away? What does it liberate? What does it hoard?

In Christ, the question I must ask of myself, Amen

May you be you. The highest of all callings.

First Cause

He holds everything together with his powerful word.
  —*Hebrews 1:3 NCV*

A greater mystery perhaps than the framing of the universe
is that you and I were chosen in Him before the foundations
of that universe. Love was first cause and God has given us just
enough explanation to unsettle us, just enough to keep us
in faith. It's part of the fabric of creation. So, in spite of what
you may believe about yourself, He has singled you out. He
has selected you from among the ages and from among worlds
and among multitudes. Love, to Him, has your face, speaks
with your voice, walks with your familiar gait, thinks the
several thoughts that you think. He loves each peculiar element
of you, beyond the excesses of His own creation, beyond the
unrimmed, chartless, and undefined limits of eternity. And
that's a lot!

In Christ, all the explanation necessary, Amen

May your life provide substantial evidence of love to those
who have lost confidence in the word itself.

Such knowledge is too wonderful for me; it is high, I cannot attain it.
—Psalms 139:6 NKJV

Part of Him is elusive, hidden, absolute *other* from us. To deny
Him mystery is to deny that which makes Him Who He is.
To wrestle with it is foolish, and too much limping Jacob.
Mystery enkindles faith, makes it necessary. And faith pleases
Him. Without the unknowable, the unexplainable, without
this unreasonableness of Him, there is little need for it. Still,
we attempt to break Him down into smaller, more discernible
parts, to dismantle the great riddle so unsettling to us, to
reduce Him to something less than He is, to penetrate the
impenetrable, to know the unknowable, as if it was our right
somehow, as if God was just another frontier of man. He has
left us one way to know Him. And that is love.

In Christ, the knowable in God, when love
needed a name to call itself, **Amen**

May love be all the understanding you need of Him.

THE PERFECT MIRROR

MARCH 24

"…In the clefts of the rock, in the secret places of the cliff, let me see your face, let me hear your voice; for your voice is sweet, and your face is lovely."—Song of Solomon 2:14 NKJV

As wax melts before the fire[5], take these plastic forms from me where I have hid myself away, the counterfeits, the disguises, the masks, the pretended forms of me. I have become a stranger to myself even in the great busyness of discovering who I am. Be my mirror, Lord—the clear, bright, and deathless image that love reflects in me. And wherever I may find You, on the lowest or the highest shelves of humanity, wherever my soul searches for You among the broken, among the weary, the lost and forgotten, or among the happy and the free, may love raise its glass to my face that I may marvel at the view.

In Christ, the perfect mirror, when love wanted to see its own face, Amen

May love in you invoke love in others, as glass to living glass, mirror to shining mirror, that Christ may arise in your midst and be reflected anywhere love has a face, a touch, or dares to speak.

5 Psalms 68, Micah 1

To Inhabit Such a World

We are fools for Christ's sake… —1 Corinthians 4:10 NCV

O, that I may inhabit such a world, so peopled and so pressed at the borders with such fools as lovers are, those who know love's deep contentment, who are awakened morning by endless morning to love's timeless suns, those with eternity fixed in the registers of their blood, whose hearts are heavy with kindness, with the lives and well being of others. O, for a world of such lovely fools, for a world of brave innocents, the beautiful and the betrothed, the healers and menders, who, impatient for heaven, summon the hereafter here and now and make a heaven of their earth.

> **In Christ,** the love that shepherds me,
> Christ, till I be surrendered and soft,
> Christ, till kindness is lord over action,
> and Christ, till I have no holds in this life,
> no claims to make, **Amen**

May you trust in the divinity and the inevitability of love.

CHRISTIANITY: AN ACT OF KINDNESS

MARCH 26

I led them with cords of human kindness, with ties of love;
I lifted the yoke from their neck and bent down to feed them.
   —Hosea 11:4 NIV

Give me fellowship with those whose Christianity itself is an act
of kindness, not an act of aggression, hostile or stern, of correction or
dominance. Set shelters about me, safe havens. Gather those about me
who sweeten the name of Christian in the thoughts of a misbelieving
and cynical world. Bind my soul to them with cords of love. Give me
those whose worship rises with them at dawn, devotion that must
express itself in generosity, in kindness, in humility, in selflessness, and
all the many things love is known by. Bring me Lord, in the midst
of such a people, such a gathering of lovely fools. Let me be counted
among them.

In Christ, the God I seek in you, Amen

May love be the warm and central hub, the sun around which
all your worlds revolve.

LOVE HAS NO AGENDA

Do everything in love.—1 Corinthians 16:14 NCV

Little in this world is done without agenda, hidden or unhidden. We labor to advance our piece up the board. It's a law of exchange we rehearse from the cradle. *But love has no agenda but love.* Fear has no place, worry has no voice, for love thinks not of itself. Love has no politics. It follows no principle, no law but its own, a law that is divine and immutable. *Christ is that law.* And love is sufficient in itself. It doesn't need anything. It doesn't labor for any gain. Love is its own reward. Here ends this little catechism.

> **In Christ,** the law of love, the rule that separates me, that calls me out, my banishment in this world, **Amen**

May you be responsible in a world of users, debtors, and defaulters, a world where truth is mere invention, something to be made up as we go along.

GOOD DAYS ARE GONNA' HAPPEN

MARCH 28

"He who would love life and see good days, let him refrain his tongue from evil, and his lips from speaking deceit."—1 Peter 3:10 NKJV

Thank God for walls, for those immovable obstacles that do not allow us to continue in some madness or some folly we get ourselves into, those that do us harm. Christ was my wall. Love was the immovable impediment I could not dance around nor outface with my words or some sharp point of my wit. Love rallied me to wellness again. It reset, retrimmed, and refitted me. I can look forward to morning and the prospects of day. I do not have to fear the mystery of it, nor my own predisposition to folly. God abides in the middlemost of my day even as He was in the night that preceded it. And God is good. Good days. They're gonna' happen. Lovers can't avoid it.

In Christ, the 'good' in good day;
Christ, my cloudless sky, Amen

May blessedness outcry and outvoice all charges, all accusations against you, real and imagined.

A Pearl of Great Price and A Pocket to Put It In

Or what will a man give in exchange for his soul?
—Mark 8:37 NKJV

Take all of your best arguments, your reason, all your assessments, judgments, all the particular elements that make you who you are. Take your faith. Take the supports by which you conduct this one life. Take all your successes and failures. Love can bring them under government, into a divine and right order. It makes ghosts of some of them and refines the rest. Love is the scale against which all things are to be weighed. And it is sufficient. If love created worlds and suspended them in nothingness, it can surely order your own. Consider an exchange. *Love is the pearl of great price and all it needs is a pocket, a big life to put it in.*

In Christ, the exchange I make, the coin I use, Amen

May any resistance, any opposition, any force in this life that labors against you, may these only accelerate the process by which champions are made, by which greatness can recognize itself, the invocation that summons up the hero in you.

AGAINST SUCH THINGS
THERE IS NO LAW

MARCH 30

But the fruit of the Spirit is love, joy, peace, longsuffering, kindness, goodness, faithfulness, gentleness, self-control. Against such there is no law.—Galatians 5:22-23 NKJV

May you love without the ornaments, without clichés, without the songs of the camp. May you love as if you mean it, not as some tribal obligation. May you love as if you invented it, as if you discovered it yourself, as gold mined from your own back yard. May you explore life with the awe of a child. May you impose love all about you today, pollinate your world with it, spread it about on the unsuspecting with what restraint, what subtlety, what liberality, what caution, or what daring love teaches you, being sure to love with no form but what the heart may give it. May love so rule you—governing body and mind, soul and sense—whatever gives you away.

In Christ, *where even nature seeks its rule,* **Amen**

May Christ be your law of life, your fixed code, the government set in the midst of you. May He be your impregnable wall, this day's ideal. May Christ be your perfect day.

A man has joy by the answer of his mouth, and a word spoken in due season, how good it is!—Proverbs 15:23 NKJV

May your words inspire, as words were first employed, having within them the breath of life and creation, light and matter. May they bring order to unordered things. May your words have the power to loose the heart of its hidden locks, the nobility to encourage and enkindle what's inside it. May your words have the power to wake some sleeping dream in its time, to wake the most Lazarus among them. And may your words have the power to enlarge life, to ennoble it, to elevate it, to affirm it, that the one upon whom they fall could wish to be no one else, that life is worth the risk of living it, that even though it spins and spins, and though it is tilted a bit on its axis, the world is beautiful because they people it and that the mystery of who we are is not a thing to fear.

In Christ, the greatest poetry, the highest English in me, Amen

Like the prophets, may your words have the charm of poetry, the weight of God.

APRIL

Christ, the resonance my soul longs for,
the deep lyric of life

You and Another Amazing
Stretch of Hours

LORD, lift up the light of Your countenance upon us.
—*Psalms 4:6 NKJV*

May God Himself be large and unmistakable, conspicuous
among those things of which you are aware today. May you
find His company easy, natural, as breath or sight. May you
fear no distances between you, however slight. May this day
be a day of elevations, of summits and heights. May the soft
and benevolent light of morning seem to linger, like a
suspended daybreak, even as one day in love, a day you knew
what it was to simply *be,* a day that demanded little thought
of how to do it, a day when nature and instinct, desire and
necessity all came together in one amazing stretch of hours,
that nothing but the good, the true, and the holy were found
among them.

In Christ, desire and necessity, Amen

May the word *amazing* never be lost in your vocabulary.

WATERS

As the deer pants for streams of water, so my soul pants for you,
O God. My soul thirsts for God, for the living God.
  —Psalms 42:1-2 NIV

In this entire psalm, all is water—every image fluid,
changing, moving, variable, mutable, unfixed, unharnessed and
unharnessable, uncontainable even as that which distresses his
soul, the God who seems to undo him with thirst and with
distance, aloof as waters. Desperation has matured in him and
his soul is a tempest, a broil of waves and waterfalls, drought
and dryness, a madness of contradictions and his only refuge is
this ecstasy, this prayer to the God of waters who has wounded
him with thirst. Life is fluid. Love is fluid, and like water, takes
many shapes, ebbs and flows, exists in a state of flood not fix,
and sets our hearts on pilgrimage and pursuit. *It is my thirst that*
satisfies. It is my hunger that feeds me. Love will understand.

In Christ, *life as thirst, love as water,* Amen

May you have the goods in you to quench the deep
thirsting of the world. May your cups be well gospelled and
overflowing.

PSALMS, HYMNS, AND
SPIRITUAL SONGS

Speak to each other with psalms, hymns, and spiritual songs, singing and making music in your hearts to the Lord.—Ephesians 5:19 NCV

It was unlike anything we had known till Him. No music of earth was so alive and so immediate, so invasive and so warm, so close and so distant at the same time. It frightened and thrilled us in the same breath. The common forms and dialects were just not high enough, nor sufficient enough to support the weight of love this genuine. Truth and warmth, passion and precision all labored together in Him to give the world something new, a language peculiar to the heart alone, that would not be learned from books, or by imitation, by rote, nor by any of the usual means. *It's all by heart. Love has no language but Christ, no tongue but Him. There's just no other translation, no other way to understand love. Love presses the heart for words and bids it speak for itself, making poets and prophets, Kings and Christs of us all.*

**In Christ, the resonance my soul longs for,
the deep lyric of life, Amen**

May your tongue be the first martyr among your expressive parts.

CHARITY

…On that day all the fountains of the great deep were broken up, and the windows of heaven were opened.—Genesis 7:11 NKJV

It's an antique, a King James relic, a word long faded with the yellowed excesses of age. It's usually found on the higher shelves of our language, all but nested away. In other words, we don't use it that much anymore. *Nonetheless, Charity itself is the very soul of Christianity. Like Christ, it's another word for love, its giving side.* Let Charity be found in you. May it be easily accessible, necessary and natural, as involuntary as blood and breath, as fluid as both. May she enjoy the company of all her siblings, Joy, Wisdom, Faith, Hope, and others of her royal sisterhood. May the house you live in be sweet with their gathered perfumes.

In Christ, Charity's first son and benefactor, Our Blessed Alms, Amen

May you discover in the simplest act of kindness the communion the soul longs for.

APRIL, SHINE YOUR ANGEL BRIGHT AND LOVELY FACE ON ME!

You crown the year with Your goodness, and Your paths drip with abundance.—Psalms 65:11 NKJV

April, shine your angel bright and lovely face on me! Be my attorney. Plead my case before a doubting world. Be my voice in this day's court. May affirmation and favor crowd itself to me and put a hush to all harm and to all the common negations that prowl about me like living things. For April is returned again, silver-winged. Her bloom enflames the earth. Her celebrating trees, a spectacle, each in its own gently tossing sphere of limbs, shaking themselves in praise. The smell of new cut grass, the boy, barefoot and greenstained, a memory in me too deep for poems. Bright April again, when the earth remembers her colors. *It's early. My brain is still dull with night and mist. Sleepless, dreamless, I woke up thirsty. My uneasiness has led me to this fountain.*

In Christ, the living metaphor of Spring, Amen

May love season your words with thawing Springs, with bright and screen-door Summers of divinity, playful and tender, innocent and sharing.

Reckless and Barefooted

April 6

But to all who did accept him and believe in him he gave the right to become children of God.—John 1:12 NCV

Once the world was as big as wonder was easy. We bolted down our halls reckless and barefooted. Adventure and exploration filled us with something electric. Innocence was mischievous and sacred. Things that seem so small to us now provoked the endless question 'why?' And we were not then afraid to ask. May wonder return to you again, childlike, fearless, primal, charged with originality and daring, the stuff of ecstasy and awe, evidence of the divine, *wonder that made it easy to believe.* May you begin to ask the questions you asked in a more curious time, in an uncivilized time, before the rod of our corrections transformed everything, that cut our playtime short, a time before we began to forget.

In Christ, my fellowship with Wonder, Amen

May you be unsettled with wonder. May it come like love itself, timeless, without conditions, innocent, playful, pure, uncivilized, sacred, reckless and barefooted.

AMONG THE WARM AND THE LIVING

So God created man in His own image; in the image of God He created him; male and female He created them.—Genesis 1:27 NKJV

You and I were created to live soul deep, to engage with life beyond the mere surface of things, to live unveiled and unguarded among the warm and the living. May love give you courage, give you eyes and sense to go with it, that you may discover life at its inner courts, that you may rediscover what is sacred, rediscover your forgotten nature, that you may traffic with those as hungry for life and love as yourself. Let your heart take the risk love will ask of it. Loose the bolts, all the hidden locks! Open wide the timid doors! Love enough to hurt for it! Allow your soul to be a trusting ambassador to love. *The human soul lives in perpetual welcome, remembering it was designed to walk with deity.*

**In Christ, my nakedness, the beauty and the strength
of my unguardedness, Amen**

May heaven smile at the first thought of you, like a doting father or mother, or a close friend. May it think of you more often than you suspect. May it sweeten your day with expectation of good. May it surround you with favor, with benefit, with joy you can't quite fit to reason or to words.

Love, The Only Wound Jesus Was Known to Inflict

April 8

Sustain me with cakes of raisins, refresh me with apples,
for I am lovesick.—Song of Solomon 2:5 NKJV

Unlike you and I, when Jesus spoke there was no obstruction
between his heart and his tongue. He was mercifully clear,
as transparent as a summer day. And just as warm. But some
could not endure the heat and walked away. For there is only
one response to Him. In love and deity it's all or nothing.
There was little left to mystery when He spoke, and what
mystery there was enkindled the heart to love. Or madness.
And I too was smitten by the only wound He was ever known to
inflict and though it was deep and unrecoverable, and though it had
the stuff of forever in it, it left no scars. He kept those to Himself.

In Christ, my incurable wound, Amen

May you understand the riddle of the wound, for your life is
now hidden in parable, in a mystery of blood and tenderness.

The following benedictions are selected from scripture. A little hint of *May* in April.

May the Lord answer you in times of trouble. *May* the God of Jacob protect you. *May* He send you help from His Temple and support you from Mount Zion. *May* He remember all your offerings and accept all your sacrifices. *May* He give you what you want and make all your plans succeed. *May* the God of hope fill you with all joy and peace in believing, that you *may* abound in hope by the power of the Holy Spirit. *May* the grace of the Lord Jesus Christ, and the love of God, and the communion of the Holy Spirit be with you all. *May* the Lord make you increase and abound in love to one another and to all, just as we do to you, so that He *may* establish your hearts blameless in holiness before our God and Father at the coming of our Lord Jesus Christ with all His saints. Now *may* the God of peace Himself sanctify you completely; and *may* your whole spirit, soul, and body be preserved blameless at the coming of our Lord Jesus Christ.

In Christ, all the above gathered in a name, Amen

LEARNING LOVE BY LOVE

APRIL 10

Let us look only to Jesus, the One who began our faith and who makes it perfect.—Hebrews 12:2 NCV

In love I am the student, even as I am the active participant, fully engaged in it and yet continually being taught and transformed, overturned and translated by it, a young Paul to love's wise and tolerant Gamaliel[6], a David to love's prophetic and intruding Nathan[7]. Learning love by love, the one rule by which I may know at last just who and what I am. Learning God within the same glad light of instruction, Whom I may know in love, Him to Whom the whole pattern, flow, and custom of my life is tending, to Whom the energies of my life may attach themselves, that I may share His life in the progress of my own. Within me are all the maps and provisions necessary.

In Christ, Who, of all I could dare to say, remains the Word that chose me, Amen

May you learn to trust when you feel nothing, when you see nothing, when you are suspended and no answers seem forthcoming.

6 *Acts 22:3*; 7 *2 Samuel 12:7*

I, therefore, the prisoner of the Lord, beseech you to walk worthy of the calling with which you were called, with all lowliness and gentleness, with longsuffering, bearing with one another in love, endeavoring to keep the unity of the Spirit in the bond of peace.—Ephesians 4:1-3 NKJV

O, if we would only indenture ourselves, make slaves of ourselves to love and to one another, that love would bloom and flourish in our midst as it did in an earlier time, when we were newly gospelled, when we were sick for it, when we were faint, overcome with love, before we forgot the sound of His voice, before we turned life itself into religion, before we grew too attached to our histories and traditions and lost our attachments to one another. If we could topple our walls, overturn our household myths, subtract from Christianity the immovable weights, the calcified and lifeless things, if we could lose all names but His. If we could mend this breach, undrive the wedge that separates us and relieve Christianity of its encumbrances, the rigging and tackle that keep it earthbound, that it may assume the very heights it did in the days of its impatient youth, when love was not so shy among us, before we came inside without being told, before there was atrophy in our wings.

In Christ, my first love remembered, old joy come back again, Amen

May you find strength in surrender. May it free what is beautiful in you.

An April Fool

"…like the morning light at dawn, like a morning without clouds. He is like sunshine after a rain that makes the grass sprout from the ground."—2 Samuel 23:4 NCV

I have learned not to be afraid of wordless days, days when it seems I have nothing in me with voice enough to rise, when the soul is shy, when I wake up, when I clear my throat and nothing happens. Then I look through the windows of morning and see the sky, silent with but a slight punctuation of clouds, the air pungent with sweetness and April, dressed with a blue you cannot name. I stare out upon it and there is no tongue, no noise in me to spoil the view. I think *what a fool I am for this.* I think what a lovely thing God does to the soul at daybreak. What a lovely thing, the soul reflecting itself in the mirror of this mid-April morning, mother and child in a fixed gaze, in wonder of each other, silent, suspended, face to face.

In Christ, my fixed and upward gaze, Amen

May love begin to disclose the lies, to unweave the fictions of your life and the many illusions that have held them together, rendering them lifeless, consigning them among voiceless and forgotten things.

LOVE, THE WORD OF GOD,
THE SO VERY WORD OF GOD

We write you now about what has always existed, which we have heard, we have seen with our own eyes, we have looked at, and we have touched with our hands. We write to you about the Word that gives life.—1 *John 1:1 NCV*

May love, like divinity made warm and visible, touchable and impossibly tender, be larger than my distractions today, be my shield, a sentinel over me, a bright angel to redeem my soul from this day's undoing, from any force that would conspire against my peace. Still to motionless nothing, all harm, mischief, all malignant intent, all unseen threats, Lord. Quiet the earth around me. Call the elements to account on my behalf. And be at peace, my soul! Ready yourself for blessedness and expectation! For He is The Ever Gracious God, your flawless rule, your benefaction, your inevitable Lord, Who orchestrates and puts to sweet music the dull and unseeming hours, Who puts time and nothingness to substance and to use, to His pleasure and to the great good of those who hope in Him.

In Christ, the so very Word of God, Love incarnate, Amen

May you find Him waiting for you among these lines, as a browser among lilies.

OF GARDENS AND LITTLE GIRLS,
OF CROSSES AND TOMBS

APRIL 14

Let us get up early to the vineyards; Let us see if the vine has budded, whether the grape blossoms are open, and the pomegranates are in bloom. There I will give you my love.—Song of Solomon 7:12 NKJV

Traffic was thick, clumsy, and creeping perilously slow. It was a beautiful afternoon. Panic seemed to have no place in such a day. But she had lost so much blood. Her mind was already slipping into a drowsy twilight. Benita had miscarried in the fourth month. It was April 14th. It is impossible to forget such a time, for it almost took her with it. One day, long after that, I could do nothing but cry. It began early and it wouldn't let up. There was no reason in it. I couldn't hold a simple conversation. I was in pain and I could not tell you why. Some time late in the day, I thought of the child we had lost, still buried in the shallow grave of my memory and still unwept. It was April 14th. I hadn't really thought about it until this day. It had been exactly one year, almost to the hour. Now it was her time. When I thought of this, tears came fresh and again, but this time deeper, from a more inward spring. It had the stuff of mourning in it, the stuff of love. I had forgotten April altogether, for that's the name we gave her. She could have no other name. *It was April, the month of gardens and little girls, of crosses and tombs, and of something she would not let me forget.*

AT THE CLOSING OF DAY

Give all your worries to Him, because He cares about you.
—1 Peter 5:7 NCV

Today is April 15th, the day we pay the fare of citizenship. But here's a thought. Why is such a deadline imposed in a season so intimate with death and resurrection? Does it have some parallel, some identification with Easter, with the Lenten fast, like the death, cleansing, and renewal that buys back our soul? Is it a restorative thing, like life again after the tolling winter? *I didn't say I had an answer, I just thought it was an interesting question.* Today is a recurring nightmare for some, a lion hidden in a thicket. For others, it's just another day that passes quietly by (having done their homework early). I'm not of the latter bunch. But take comfort in this: *Love is sufficient and will remain long after the nations dissolve into history. Only love matters at the closing of day, at the conclusion of this odd masterpiece of life and citizenship. Love, if it is to make sense at all.*

In Christ, the sense we make of it, Amen

May alarm find no place in your day, no appointment, no door of entry.

APRIL 16

He must increase, but I must decrease.—John 3:30 NKJV

I worship an invisible God. He has a name I cannot say.
I long for and await a heaven I cannot see. I am commanded
to imitate Him and yet to do this is to become invisible as
He is, to lose myself in love, for hiddenness to become the
greater part of who I am, to be guilty of acts that are unseen
of kindnesses to which no name can be applied. For love at
its truest is selfless, nameless, invisible. And I am taken up, ear
raptured, seen no longer before the watching world. The gre
paradox is that love while making me invisible, tells me who
I am, sorts me out, defines me, strips away illusion and
pretension and gives me my truest dimensions in a world of
pretenders.

In Christ, the invisible God made visible in me, Amen

May you vanish in love, dissolve into love's greater self.

LOVER'S CATECHISM: UNDER COMMAND

I can of Myself do nothing. As I hear, I judge; and My judgment is righteous, because I do not seek My own will but the will of the Father who sent Me.—John 5:30 NKJV

As all LOVERS who would come after Him, Christ lived under command. He did nothing outside the limits given Him by His father. Love was His legal jurisdiction, the clear margin within which Christ kept Himself. He did nothing that was 'not love.' Every action, every reflex, was under the sole command of love. Love was the God over, in, and through Him. It was the God over God. And He was free to weep, free to rage. He was free with a freedom the earth had yet to know. He was free to grieve with all the passion in Him, free to laugh without restraints, from some deep place within Him, to feel, to be moved, to be shaken, to be disturbed deeply in His spirit. He was free to be fully and authentically human, with all the miracle that accompanies it, and to express divinity in its time, when love, wonder, and necessity gave their mutual consents.

In Christ, where humanity and divinity meet and agree, Amen

May you live daily where He delights the most.

LOVER'S CATECHISM:
LOVERS ARE A HOLY PEOPLE

APRIL 18

The LORD will establish you as a holy people to Himself, just as He has sworn to you, if you keep the commandments of the LORD your God and walk in His ways. —Deuteronomy 28:9 NKJV

To live a life in love is to live a holy life, a life with all the usual complications subtracted from it. All things revolve and orbit about one single deathless sun. Love elevates life and LOVERS live the big picture. It's what love does to the vision. The particular details and the weak arguments that burden the rest of us are nonissues to those who truly love. Being holy is being like Him Who is first a LOVER, always God.

In Christ, the big picture, Amen

May your soul be restored to the beauty of its origins. May it be cleansed of its former life, leaving only a vague remembrance that death ever lived there or had any dominion at all.

LOVER'S CATECHISM:
DON'T MAKE THE LOVER THINK

APRIL 19

Turn your eyes away from me, for they have overcome me.
—*Song of Solomon 6:5 NKJV*

Intimacy doesn't think. It's too overwhelmed, too engaged,
the cloud too thick for words or the distractions of thought.
Don't make the LOVER think. Does God think? Does He
have to work things out? I suspect not. His work is done.
And the LOVER may enjoy continual Sabbath in his Beloved.
So don't bother him with your theology, with the study of
unstudiable things. He won't engage in your debates. He's not
attracted to them. There's no reflection for him to see in the
glass. It's unattractive to him. Scripture itself is a lyric to the
LOVER. He doesn't look for argument in it. He doesn't look
for his proofs there. He thinks he's listening to music. Leave
him alone.

In Christ**, the music I hear, the wine of LOVERS, **Amen

When you consider your former life, the one before love,
may it seem as but a dream, one easily forgotten as when you
awakened from that dream.

ISN'T SHE BEAUTIFUL?

I was in the Spirit on the Lord's Day...—Revelation 1:10 NKJV

I got to church late. It was full that morning, so I stood in
the back next to a friend and two of her daughters. In a more
informal moment in the service, my son's wife, Katie, a few
months pregnant with our first grandchild, walked back to
where I stood and put her arms around me. I can't remember
if there were any words. Having been distracted all morning,
suddenly I was overwhelmed. As she walked away, I turned
to our friend. With tears in my eyes and some obstruction
in my throat, I said, "Isn't she beautiful?" Worship continued,
but somehow more alive, glorious, and tearfully sweet. Love
had caught me up unsuspecting and swept me from myself.
*When I think about what Christianity should be, what life should
be, what life and faith should be giving back to us, when I think about
what is truly sacred, I know it was all there, in that brief exchange
with my daughter-in-law. And if I could condense that, distill it into
words, if I could bottle it, like ink or perfume, put it in a pill, or
compress it into one astounding book, that's what you'd be holding
in your hands at this moment, not this imitation, this exercise
in pomp and scribble.*

WHAT IS IT ABOUT YES THAT YOU DON'T UNDERSTAND?

I will betroth you to me forever; I will betroth you in righteousness and justice, in love and compassion.—Hosea 2:19 NIV

When all creation gathered as in one voice and cried out to a Holy God, "Do you love me?" Christ was the answer He gave, the YES it so desperately wanted to hear. *So what is it about YES that confounds you? What is it about YES that you don't understand? This word sweeter than mercy, warmer than the fires of home, this Grace of YES, so royal, so divine, so deathless, and so near! Would you remain asleep and but dream of love? Would you settle for the imagination of the thing and not the thing itself? O, that we would become a people of YES, without denials, without refusals, affirming love in all things, drinking deep of life to its fullest, most irresistible measures.*

Always YEShua, the Christ of promise, YES as it gathers in the mouth of God, Amen

May your one life affirm something true before an uncertain world.

But One Death More,
One Martyrdom Between Us

April 22

"Will you lay down your life for My sake?"—John 13:38 NKJV

Let argument within you die. Give it no tongue, no disguise, no residence, no altar, no politics, no familiar council, no sanctuary, no fertile ground, no water for its thirst. Give it no place to feed and nothing to feed upon. May it have no memory. May it have no steward, no nurse. May love sweeter the mind and quiet the soul with good report. How we wast ourselves! And on nothing. How the dark lords laugh and mock at the loss, at a people estranged from themselves. *But O, how close is love. But one death more, one martyrdom between us, one heaven that waits in eager reply to the great question I see within you.*

Till Him, Amen

May your house be a house of peace, a house without locks, not a religious place where arguments are raised, venerated, and protected, where lines are considered, weighed, drawn ar defended, but a holy place, a hallowed place where stillness and light may give freely of the divinity within them.

That's Good Jesus!

For as many of you as were baptized into Christ have put on Christ.
  —*Galatians 3:27 NKJV*

It's not improper for me to say, *'I am here to love and not to be loved.'* It's within the bounds of a higher law to say that *loving is greater than being loved,* just as *giving is greater than receiving,* that being loved is not the reward, but the loving itself. Yet in this strange, efficient, and beautiful economy of love I can expect a return on the least parcel of my investment. *That's good theology. That's good Jesus!*

**In Christ, the loving itself, Christ, the investment
I am to make, Amen**

May kindness be the response in you where such a response is not expected. May gentleness have the power to overrule an offense and the power to heal.

APRIL 24

I will sing to the LORD, because He has dealt bountifully with me.
  —*Psalms 13:6 NKJV*

May the sweetness of the Lord overwhelm you today. May it
come like dominion, in bold strides. May it overrun fatigue,
countermand stubborn doubt and other corruptions of belief,
put dread and annoyance to flight. May the fact that HE IS be
sufficient. May it be just cause for celebration, for joy that makes
long hours brief, that makes industry effortless, that sustains the
heart through the lag end of day. May He be inescapable, as in
some unexpected triumph you cannot attribute to anything
but Him, some unreasonable, irrepressible, irrevocable good.
May those things that would normally bring sorrow be
translated, as in a shared perception with deity, that you may see
purely, as love sees; love that gives new and promising, and more
hopeful shapes to grief. And may your big life conform itself
to His composition, your eager clay to His detail, to His most
lovely idea of you.

In Christ, my inescapable, unreasonable, irrepressible,
and irrevocable good, Amen

May the above serve you gladly and well. Today and everyday!

DON'T LET A DAY GO BY
WITHOUT ONE

You gave me life and showed me kindness, and in your care you watched over my life.—Job 10:12 NCV

Lord, let kindness be sovereign in all my actions. May love leave its imprint on all that I chance to do and in all You assign. For I believe that a simple act of kindness moves Your heart more than we have suspected, especially the hidden ones, the invisible ones, the ones that only You may enjoy. Receive them as worship, for they are better than our songs, more powerful than oaths and creeds. May praise rise in the heart of my deeds, silent, selfless, and sweet to You, O Lord. May it flow from a grateful place in me. May I, in some small parcel, return to You that kindness first showed to me. Help me to rethink what is truly important, where the eye of love watches closest. And may we fill our days full with them, with little acts of kindness. May we not look upon any day in the absence of them, for they bring You, O God, into our exchanges.

In Christ, the kindness of God shown in an act, **Amen**

May you live in the gratitude of that kindness first showed to you.

MAN OF SORROWS, GOD OF LOVE

APRIL 26

He was despised, and rejected of men…—Isaiah 53:3 ASV

The word never came up in conversation. It came all by itself some time later. It's just not something that was told to me upon my first inquiries into this faith. *Sorrow* has lost its place in our modern school of spirituality. It doesn't sell. It's a thing to be 'fixed' in someone. For the affluence of this latter age has told us different things about ourselves. And we have believed every pleasant report. *Lord, You said hard things to us. The flame of love burned too close, too deep. The loathing we felt for ourselves we turned against You. You came as heaven's own personal invitation and yet rejection was written upon You, and in distinguishing marks. You have not made it easy for us and we have always despised what we do not understand. Yet I want to know You, to feel what You feel, to see what You see, to weep over that which makes You weep, to love what You love, to embrace sorrow when it comes and know the wonder hidden in its heart and not be afraid, so I may wear upon my body the fragrance, the myrrh, the lover's perfume.*

In Christ, Who took my sorrows as if they were important to Him, Amen

May your own tears soften the stubborn clay and make mortality moldable again.

Beyond Human Likeness

Just as there were many who were appalled at him, his appearance was so disfigured beyond that of any man and his form marred beyond human likeness...—Isaiah 52:14 NIV

If we love, we must be willing to love to the extent of our own ruin and then some. If we love, death is no impediment. If we love, we must be willing to love to our own debasement, to the exclusion of all other things human and natural, reasonable and civilized. Love engages divinity within us, giving us the strength to realize the conditions listed above. Israel had become but a frightful caricature of herself. She was as one beaten, as one whose pulpy, bruised and misshapen form no longer resembled the thing it had been. She no longer could boast the beauty in which God had taken delight in her alone. In love, Christ took upon Himself her distorted features. He was beaten, shaped into her unrecognizable form. In Him, heaven held up a mirror that she could see herself. But she turned away for she could not bear what she saw.

In Christ, love beyond human likeness, Amen

May the love that fulfilled the law be your law.

APRIL 28

He is not here; for He is risen, as He said.—Matthew 28:6 NKJV

O, Bright Child! Roused early of a Sunday morning, a Sunday dressed in white raiment, a day of linen and lilies. O, that I may set my course by that same deathless and new risen star, Him I know, Who has wielded my soul about in too many dreamless passages of night, Him Who has rescued me from beneath the lifeless shroud of my captivity. O, Deathless Easter, April of my rebirth! My one and lovely day of Awe and Thankfulness! My day in Him alone Who is the Alpha, the First of Light, the First of Lovers, my close and kindred God, radiant and earth redeeming Son of Majesty and Mystery.

In Christ, our perennial Spring, Amen

May the word 'old' never apply to you, even as it can never be applied to Christ Himself. 33 was a good year.

ABOVE ALL THINGS

And above all things have fervent love for one another.
  —1 Peter 4:8 NKJV

Love is our best proof of an inward life in God. Love is what He
has deposited in us, that divine bit of Himself, in a place far
beyond the reaches of our own authority or control, where
the deep engines of life are kept. And we are to no less than
burn with love for one another. Remember those films about
the Titanic and all those guys in her deep cellars, where the
furnace sweats and rages and the engine grinds? They're all
shirtless, wet with grime and toil, shovels in their hands,
stoking the great heat. Okay, bad choice of ships, but you
get the idea.

In Christ, *where the deep engines of life are kept, Christ,*
how I choose to love, **Amen**

May love have absolute jurisdiction in you.

LAMENT AT THE CLOSE OF APRIL

APRIL 30

...Like a lily among thorns, so is my love among the daughters.
—Song of Solomon 2:2 NKJV

I've enjoyed this month. I've had fun with the name itself. I'm smitten by it. *I am April's fool.* This daily devotional has been easier too, as if my hours were shortened, as if the work has been taken out of it, for April comes with celebration and tribute, her gowns are flowing white, gilded lightly at the seams. She does as easy to language what she does to the earth She calls back the color, the majesty, miracle and mirth. She is the poet among the twelve, the first of females, the younger sisters May, June, and July following after. She is perfumed and playful, exuberant, flirtatious. She's not afraid to laugh out loud, or to blush with maiden color. She is lovely with youth. Her journals are laden with poems, songs of the waking Spring, the music of resurrection and life again, of promise that pollinates the heart with hope, hope that is Easter Morning bright, warm at the anticipation of each new sun.

In Christ, the deathless April, Amen

If someone grins at you unexpectedly, may you find something sacred about it.

MAY

Christ, all that love commands of me

MAY: THE HEALER
AMONG THE SEASONS

MAY 1

For lo, the winter is past, the rain is over and gone. The flowers appear on the earth; the time of singing has come, and the voice of the turtledove is heard in our land.—Song of Solomon 2:11-12 NKJV

The year has blown itself out of all extremes and has brought us mercifully around to her again, to May, the bright crown of Spring. A healer among the seasons, she helps you forget. She helps you remember. She has properties to re-create. Her world is green and bulges with promise. Her weather, mild and accommodating. Invitation and welcome is everywhere. We open our windows again. We hear the buzz of tiny winged life just outside our screen doors and among the honey rich blossoms. She invites us to our porches where we can rock to the drowsy hum of time and cradle ourselves in the opiates of sunset. We hear again the muted laughter of children in the distance, a riot of giggles, and watch the bees labor among the juicy blooms.

In Christ, the Spring of all our calendars, Amen

May this season be pleasant company to you, like easy conversation or poetry that doesn't make you work for it, music that lengthens your hours with singing.

TILL HIM

The path of the righteous is like the first gleam of dawn, shining ever brighter till the full light of day.—Proverbs 4:18 NIV

Have you ever considered that love is the only reason you're here at all? That it's what we've been given this brief mortality for? Unseen divinity in our midst shaping us, preparing us for itself? That this life is but a courtship, a special season in the school of love that has but a certain span of determined days, a Christianity whose end is consummation, now but a step, perhaps one death from us, a romance that makes all life about us sacred? So we live in a certain suspense, as lovers do, suspense that filters deep into the pores of life, that seeps beneath the polish of our surfaces, that rouses adoration at its spring, that sets devotion adrift in the rivers of the blood, that overflows the heart until it sings. *The result is worship. It's what we have till Him.*

In Christ, Him I await, Him I now live, Amen

Till Him, may love continue its refinements in the heart. May heaven itself stir within you like a thing unborn, like life within life.

MAY 3

But Martha was distracted…—Luke 10:40 NKJV

Life is complex enough and still most of it is spent in processing noise and other distractions, or being merchants, fixers. *Spent* is the keyword. We have a failing economy where love is currency. Our finances are chaos. There is unevenness, an imbalance that is hard to reconcile in the neglect and mismanagement. Love gets complicated or is altogether aloof. It becomes too much work because it usually gets what little is left of us after the account is drained. *I am overwhelmed, Lord. I have too little, much too little to return to You Who demands so very all of me, Who demands the surrender of every unaccounted part, yet there is little left when the accounting is done. I live but a half life that is not life at all. I am as bitter as Martha in my laboring. I am vexed by the Mary that I refuse of myself.*

In Christ, my reconcilement, my one and true distraction, Amen

May love have no impediments, no barriers, nothing that would steal the slightest part of you away or fret your soul to withdraw itself inward.

MAY 4

Owe no one anything except to love one another, for he who loves another has fulfilled the law.—Romans 13:8 NKJV

Give em' love! Give em' everything you've got! Keep the three syllable gospel warm on your lips, the 'I love you' that elevates life! Keep this simplest of all testaments active and current! Learn to love the risk love asks of you! Let the heart break easy and love the pain! Rejoice over what's missing of it, over every shard and splinter that cannot be recalled! Unnail the Jesus in you! Empty your bins, your hoarded gold! Give from your most treasured stores, from the deep reserve where death has no voice, no key of entry, no password, where fear has no presence, no claims, no rights at all and cannot cripple, stall, nor delay love. Leave no legacy but love! Love that echoes longer than your money. Grieve hard! Love long! Die broke!

In Christ, all that love commands of me, **Amen**

May you be touchable proof of love in a world of Thomas.

A HAPPY DAY OF
RIOTS & PERMISSIONS

MAY 5

Open my eyes to see the miracles in your teachings.
  —*Psalms 119:18 NCV*

May wonder, amazement, and the expectation of miracles start
a riot in your soul, irrevocable, irrepressible, even from the first
hint of light upon your hills. For such things I think daybreak
was made for, when dreams are grown ripe for harvest in the
dark and benevolent cradles of night. And Brother Sun, may he
come upon you today and fill your soul with promise, sweet as
midsummer, bright as crowned majesty, with love that gave
him his beginnings, that spoke him in place in one happy riot
of speech, that gave him fellowship with the stars, with all the
lesser lights, and with multitudes before you and I, love that
gave him worlds to shine upon and warmth enough to cover
your happy little universe.

In Christ, all permissions granted, Amen

May you suspect something good to come to you. May you
give yourself all the permissions necessary. May suspicion, too
sweet to ignore, dominate your thoughts and with a soft and
benevolent light lay gentle siege to all the remote and lonely
reaches of your meditations and hush all your common care.

The words of the LORD are pure words, like silver tried in a furnace of earth, purified seven times.—Psalms 12:6 NKJV

If I could say but one true thing, one honest report that would resonate like music, like poetry you swear you heard once when the heart was still and unsuspecting, that dizzied the sense with light and celebration, that would now speak redeeming volumes to a distracted world. O, if I could invoke to this mute page one small share of divinity and reclaim that heaven we sold so casually for a loaf of bread and a song. O, if ink were tears. If words could weep.

**In Christ, where ink and ecstasy seek
each other's company in me, Amen**

May you acquire an ear for music, that you may hear Him when He calls. And may He call to you with a lover's voice.

WHERE WE FIND OUR FEET
IN A DIZZY WORLD

MAY 7

For where your treasure is, there your heart will be also.
  —*Matthew 6:21 NKJV*

May Christ be your center of gravity, your unavoidable
attraction, your centermost pulse, the Genesis core, your
source of life and beginnings. May He be your warm
middle-earth where oaths are bred and kept, where the light
of counsel burns, about which all things revolve and seek
their equilibrium, where we find our feet in a dizzy world.

In Christ, my center of gravity, my good balance, Amen

May love confer upon you something irresistible, something
deeply attractive outside of beauty, a magnetism against which
there are no arguments, stronger than nature itself, that even
the dullest lead cannot resist.

Till Blessedness Rules the Heart

"Do not remember the former things, nor consider the things of old. Behold, I will do a new thing, now it shall spring forth; shall you not know it? I will even make a road in the wilderness and rivers in the desert."—Isaiah 43:18-19 NKJV

May Blessedness lay happy siege to your little kingdom. May it wear down your defenses against it. May it find you yielded, willing. May it give you new histories to look back upon. May it give new shapes to your thoughts and to the words that give them away. May your next encounter with life, your next exchange with warm humanity, your next evaluation of things, your next opinion, including those we make of ourselves, may it shine with the sweet generous light of Beatitude. All this, till Blessedness rules the heart.

In Christ, Blessedness in the rich fertile centers of life, Amen

May you have all that is yours by a promise, by a living inheritance, all that grows even now in the greenhouse of your expectations, that dwells safely in the mystery of God, the sacred storehouse of Him Who keeps our days and hours to Himself, Who releases blessing in its season, in the mellow dropping Fall known only to Him. May you be close to the tree.

LOVER'S CATECHISM: LOVERS ARE KIND

MAY 9

Love suffers long and is kind…—1 Corinthians 13:4 NKJV

Love is kind and with a kindness that is alive with divinity, a kindness that shares the greater qualities of love itself, being first royal, absolute, unfailing, without agenda, without a hidden design, selfless, easy, prolific, boundless, generous, not overbearing but rightly balanced, spontaneous, true, effective, and friendly. *Lord, let kindness find residence in me and language that it may express itself, that it may liberate the divine within me, that it may filter into all my habits and in all places where life meet. life. Let it be warm with a warmth that brings the lost sense of touch back into our world. Give me eyes that weep at the very word itself. Let kindness labor within me till I am transfigured, till it shines upon my face with an eager light, an irresistible, inviting, casual light. Let me toil and let me rest within its shades. Let it be the watchman at my lips. Let it keep vigil in the council where my thoughts debate with themselves.*

In Christ, if warmth be found in me and if it has a name, Amen

May you know the heroism in a simple act of kindness.

Lover's Catechism:
Lovers are Irresistible

*And walk in love, as Christ also has loved us and given Himself
for us, an offering and a sacrifice to God for a sweet-smelling aroma.*
   —*Ephesians 5:2 NKJV*

Love is the Christ-sufficient life. Warm, yielded, touchable, divine
and yet deeply and uniquely human, possessing vision that is
true, dependable, clear and unspoiled. It's freedom that is truly
free. It's innocence transfigured, renewed to the beauty of
its origins. And this is only the beginning. How could such
a thing not be irresistible? Those few who find it want little
else in this life. They too are irresistible. *Lord, I want to love
like that! With love that is larger than dreams, more prevailing than
my refusals and my complaints. Let my circle of love be no less an
expanse, a universe in itself, containing worlds, multitudes, suns, and
stars to people my skies. O, for such love as this!*

In Christ, *what is truly attractive, beautiful in any of us,* **Amen**

May you learn again to weep, to grieve, to surrender
completely in the might of compassion. May heaven give
you a gospel that listens as well as it speaks.

LOVER'S CATECHISM:
LOVERS ARE EASY

MAY 11

Come unto me, all ye that labour and are heavy laden, and I will give you rest. Take my yoke upon you, and learn of me; for I am meek and lowly in heart and you will find rest for your souls. For my yoke is easy and my burden is light.—Matthew 11:28-30 KJV

LOVERS make easy work of life around them. They take the work out of human exchange. You like being around them. Even nature seems to be in agreement. Birds and other small creatures, with their high strung little alarms seem at peace with the LOVER. Rain is but a percussive and liquid poetry. A LOVER is free to be themselves and invite all to do the same. Fearless in innocence, they assume the best in everyone, giving and accepting without exclusion, not extracting interest or usury for they do not merely loan, but give themselves away.

In Christ, *the good life, my ease, my deep repose,* **Amen**

Life is complicated enough. May love help you reverse this process.

The LORD shall preserve your going out and your coming in from this time forth, and even forevermore.—Psalms 121:8 NKJV

May harm be worlds away. May blessing impose itself upon you, easy as April. May good, benefit, pleasance, and peace itself find a direct course to you, by quick means, bringing quiet celebration to the heart, thankfulness to the speech. May this day give you spoils you did not seek. May pressure loose the champion in you. May all your mirrors be kind, especially the living ones. May the ending day say good things of you. May it close with an applaud of color in your sky. *And above all these things, may love be the first obligation in you. May the rest come easy.*

In Christ, *the obligation we bring to our world,* **Amen**

May love grant you a heroic life.

CHRISTIANITY IS A ROMANCE:
ACT ACCORDINGLY

MAY 13

My beloved is mine, and I am his: he feedeth among the lilies.
  —*Song of Solomon 2:16 KJV*

If Christianity were a book, it would be a romance.
A good read, it begins as courtship and goes the way all
good courtships go, to an altar, to the ecstasies and to the
unimaginable life that follows. We are His other self, the
counterpart. What is our own personal testimony but a love
story? So enjoy your Christianity, beloved, whatever your
story may be. It's romance. Act accordingly. It's much more
fun that way.

**In Christ, this weakness in my knees,
the wine in my blood, Amen**

May love in you express itself first in meekness, where
servanthood and divinity meet. A Christ event in the life
of faith.

MAY: COULD SUCH A MONTH
HAVE ANY OTHER NAME?

Cling to what is good.—Romans 12:9 NKJV

If April opens the door, MAY is permission to enter. MAY is allowance, permission, approval, sanction, assent. MAY is the soothing YES the soul is crazy for. Like a child in line at the carnival whose heart is full to excess and ecstasy, suspense and overthrow, like deity in you anxious to express itself, coming and going, giving and receiving, like the scent of a flower you can almost name stealing soft through our screen doors in the sweet breath of Spring, this delicious word MAY, whether it be poised on the lips like a kiss or a prayer, if it labors in the mind against some doubt or misbelief, or if it be dizzy with celebration in the heart, *love will not be exhausted of it. Could such a month have any other name?*

In Christ, *life as interpreted in the Spring,* Amen

Of her for whom this month derives its name, MAY she give you 31 days of her generosity, of her warmth, her medicines, her affirmations and agreements, and the harmony that sweetens the score of your big life.

MAY LOVE FIND A MOMENT IN YOU

MAY 15

Now the purpose of the commandment is love from a pure heart, from a good conscience, and from sincere faith…—1 Timothy 1:5 NKJV

May your faith make deep sense to you today, and therefore, be little work. May love find its height in response. May you remember the language that has nothing to do with words and everything to do with love. *May you become fluent, articulate in the use of it.* May you remember the Christianity that has nothing to do with words and everything to do with love. *May you become fluent, articulate in the use of it.* May love conspire in your behalf. May you always live in the sweet suspicion and expectation of love. May love find a moment in you today. Maybe two.

In Christ, the beautiful life, Amen

May Christ be the only distance between you and an unimaginable life.

May and Thankfulness: They Were Made for Each Other

For all things are for your sakes, that grace, having spread through the many, may cause thanksgiving to abound to the glory of God.
—*2 Corinthians 4:15 NKJV*

This marriage was made in heaven. There is a generous bond between these two words, *may* and *thankfulness. May* with her permissions, her grants, her approvals, her invitations. *Thankfulness* with its grace, its gratitudes, its resonance of divinity. They enjoy each other's company and like all good marriages, they produce some unforgettable offspring. May thankfulness rule in all your exchanges. May it be an inseparable part of you. May it bring lightness to your mind, pleasance to your voice. May the language come easy. May it be a welcomed presence between you and others, between you and your own soul. May it be a key that unlocks something beautiful in someone. May thankfulness be the good habit in the order of your days, a trusting companion in all your appointments. May you be warm with it. You get the idea!

In Christ, my thankfulness, Amen

May thankfulness give you audience with God, for I suspect it's a thing He delights in.

THE TRUEST POETRY OF LOVE

MAY 17

Give ear, O heavens, and I will speak; and hear, O earth, the words of my mouth.—*Deuteronomy 32:1 NKJV*

Love needs no unnecessary ornament, nor does it need the burden of too much thought. Simple as Jesus, deep as Christ, let love speak for itself! Open your mouth and let the heart unfold itself in an audible bloom! **"I love you."** It's that easy. Don't think! Just say it! May your soul ache with sweetness till it rises to the lips like the Psalm of Life. May it be like a need newly kindled, a hunger awakened in you, your Christianity evolving, expanding, exploring new limits of itself, breaking free of its old restraints. And in the moment it comes, may you recognize it, that lull in a conversation, that little unsettled thing in the middle of you, the ignition of tiny flames, the slight tremor in the voice, the truest poetry of love.

> ***In Christ,*** *when we mean what we say, Christ,*
> *what is genuine in love,* ***Amen***

May your faith be enjoyable to you and to those around you. May it be inviting, irresistible, lovely with mystery, warm like love itself. May your faith be a tree with a swing on it. May it be ice cream with extra spoons.

As Only You Can Hear

The deep closed around me; weeds were wrapped around my head. I went down to the moorings of the mountains; the earth with its bars closed behind me forever; yet You have brought up my life from the pit, O LORD, my God. "When my soul fainted within me, I remembered the LORD; and my prayer went up to You, into Your holy temple."—Jonah 2:5-7 NKJV

When prayer closes up in me, when the spring is dry, when I am hollow and artless inside, when the deep vents are sealed shut, when the odd man is reflected in my mirrors, when passion is indiscriminate and has little rule, when music in me has lost its conviction and I am tumbled down from its heights, when I am reduced to the basement depths of myself, I know You can yet hear me, out of this impossible tangle of speech, outside the corridors of sense, outside art and imagining. Hear me as only You can hear, for I am set beneath all detectable thresholds. I am mute as waters. But my soul is resonant, sufficient with Jonah.

In Christ, the voice that rises at the end of words, Amen

May love wash you clean of this world. May this world become the Pilate that washes its hands of you at last.

LOVE: A STRONG TOWER
IN A DAY OF BABBLE

MAY 19

Therefore its name is called Babel, because there the LORD confused the language of all the earth.—*Genesis 11:9 NKJV*

May this day come sweet to the ear with good things. May benediction and all good tidings seek you out. In the rising murmur and gossip of the streets, may you detect the good, the worthy, the honest, the holy, the sincere. May your senses be dull to the voices that would diminish you, even if one of them happens to be your own. May you hear what love has to say to you today and may you be large enough to believe. May you be ever vigilant, cautious, watchful, for those unbelieving and faithless that would steal the music from you or pluck the color from your day. May love be your argument against a world of smallness and petty feeders. May love be your strong tower in the day of Babble.

> **In Christ, my world ordered aright,
> my ear sweet with good report, Amen**

May you be willing to unlearn.

But there is a spirit in man, and the breath of the Almighty gives him understanding.—Job 32:8 NKJV

God will not be reduced to anything, not to a word, an idea, a theology, or to a trick of human logic. He's too elusive for that. It has always been His intent, rather, to elevate us, not for us to diminish Him. Faith itself must furnish what understanding cannot and yet it gives us no tongue to satisfy our craving to know. Language itself cannot reach so high or deep. But love can. Love is sufficient in itself and love is as close as it comes to understanding that which even faith denies us.

In Christ, *if we are to understand at all, Amen*

May you not weary of what is elusive about God, what is incontainable, ineffable, or incomprehensible in Him, for He sustains His mystery, and sets the soul to pilgrimage and pursuit. *To love is to know Him. And love is sufficient.*

May 21

…Love does not parade itself, is not puffed up; does not behave rudely, does not seek its own, is not provoked, thinks no evil…
—*1 Corinthians 13:4-5 NKJV*

Pride, a sightless, reckless pilot, as blind as dirt, it sees no farther than its own image. Love is 'otherness,' sublime and considerate, holy and effective. It is a purified 'selflessness,' the divine and dread *anti-me*. Love and pride are incompatibles. Pride is a pirate, a thief, a pillager, a usurper. It 'puffs' itself up, only for love to hide itself away in aloofness, leaving pride to its own sad and lonely spectacle. Till invitation, humility, and sincerity bid love welcome again.

In Christ, *the self I never knew till love,* **Amen**

May you grieve over your pride till your soul renounces it.

HEAVEN—A MEMORY
DISGUISED AS A PRAYER

I will give you the keys of the kingdom of heaven...
—Matthew 16:19 NCV

We colored pictures of it while the adults were upstairs
churching themselves with mystery and singing, singing we heard
through thick walls and ceilings so impossibly high above us. Our
harps were uneven and crayon brown. Our angels, those plump
little cherubs, naked and smiling with ruddy and compact little
faces peeking over a bank of clouds, were fleshed with pink and
topped with yellow hair. We could not then stay so easily within
the lines. We were children. But I grew up. Heaven was left
behind, among the other myths and legends of my childhood.
I blew away those clouds with cool blasts of reason and high
argument. Until love. *Lord, You brought heaven to my lonely earth.*
You gave love charge over me and with it gave me back the heaven of my
youth. Love, be my rule, my reward, the heaven I enjoy in the rightness
of life, in the Christ I follow. I am Your harp to play upon. With warm
rule, keep time within my breast and all my lovely colors within the lines.

In the name of Christ, itself a heaven, Amen

If you are ever asked to describe heaven, may love be all the
explanation you can think of.

OF POINTING NATHANS
AND DEAD URIAHS

MAY 23

Have mercy upon me, O God…—Psalms 51:1 NKJV

In a time of pointing Nathans and dead Uriahs, love incited David to words, to the psalm growing within him. Grief was full, round-wombed. Sorrow was demanded to speak, to deliver itself up, for the time had come to unsecret the heart, to free him from the unbearable levy upon his soul. And he cried at last, "I'm sorry!" *Your love, O Lord, was greater than his offense. It is greater than my own. Grief broke out in words, but You only heard singing, a hymn of absolution precious to Your ears.*

In Christ, the psalm that grows within me, my defense in a time of pointing Nathans and dead Uriahs, Amen

May love dispel any unkindness bound in memory, any injury, any unforgiven or unresolved thing, any regret, any petty forgeries of the small or unbelieving, any impurity that revels in the mind, that chokes the vital breath, that banishes the heart from its higher life, that would extinguish the flame of divinity within you or quiet its voice.

With my soul I have desired You in the night, Yes, by my spirit within me I will seek You early…—Isaiah 26:9 NKJV

4:30 a.m. I have come empty again into this little room, this world within my world, population 01, to debate with silence as if it were a living thing. I have crept out unseen from under the veiled lids of night, my house silent as a windless sea. And I think it is good to be here. There is a clarity before morning breaks with light, when quiet overrules the senses. Necessity, like an inward compass, leads me here where I may loose my soul to a trust of words and stillness. *There is a prayer ever poised upon the lips of morning.*

In Christ, my silent night, my Bethlehem at daybreak, Amen

May morning give you words. May you have all of them you need, all that is sufficient and all that is good, in right measure for this day's trade, as your soul disperses itself, as it invites a world inward, as you mete yourself out in the exchange.

THE DREAM OF LOVE

...Lovers of pleasure rather than lovers of God, having a form of godliness but denying its power.—*2 Timothy 3:4-5 NKJV*

It topples kingdoms. It gives passion its heat. Poets feed on it. It ignites the warm rush that circumnavigates the body, that sends mad pulses to the brains of lovers. *The dream of love.* And yet, when love is understood in such a way that Self is seated in the center of it, when love is thought of as but an emotional investment with promise of return, when passion is its argument, when it is balanced and weighed against my own satisfaction, it is no longer love, but only some imagined likeness of it, a mutation, a counterfeit, a dream, *having a form of godliness but...* For these unfortunate reasons, most of us feed at an empty table, upon some adolescent and unsubstanced dream of love, dreaming of feasts and waking up hungry.

In Christ, *wakefulness at the end of dreams,* **Amen**

May love enlarge your expectations, give shape and dimension to your dreams, not for things of this world, but for the immense God, even He that inhabits your inner spaces and gives substance to hope.

ROMANCE IS FOR GROWN-UPS

And what I say to you, I say to all: Watch!—Mark 13:37 NKJV

There are clouds that brood above us, thick, dark, and menacing, heavy with unborn thunder, rain, and mystery, a thing that is lovely to me. The threat is no less present, and yet the beauty silences the danger. The trick is in the watch. Gazing for too long a time at such a sky is not altogether wise. Especially if you are walking on water. Romance is for grown-ups. Though it brings out something untamed in each of us, romance is for big people. *O, how intolerably close we are to a table prepared for feasting, and yet want so for bread. How childish are our refusals. And how lonely we remain. How we unknowingly mock our own souls. How cool and aloof we are in a world so wanting for warmth and for a mirror to see something true in ourselves. Watch, my soul. Be vigilant, my heart. Summon your little strength. And call upon Him Whom you love.*

In Christ, Him I love, Amen

From the inmost to the extremes, from those base instincts to the higher ones, the body, the passions, all those meditations that frequent the mind, where thoughts stir with life, wherever darkness contends with light, may love be master, the Absolute in a world that has stricken Absolute from the record.

All of Love's Exchanges are Intimate

May 27

He tends his flock like a shepherd: He gathers the lambs in his arms and carries them close to his heart; he gently leads those that have young.—Isaiah 40:11 NIV

Intimacy, to Christ, was a natural response to all life as it gathered around Him. Eden walking about in sandaled feet, reclaiming the earth again. Nakedness and innocence, truth and loveliness at home with itself. *Intimacy is all love knows. Love looks close when it looks at all. Every soul a mirror. Every heart a home.* Christ was human, deeply human, human from some forgotten order of human, perfect man, for our truest humanity expresses itself with such hints of the divine, a humanity that makes love easy, natural, and makes obedience to His command so little work. Call it by the name of Christian if you choose. Still, many walked away from Him, puzzled, angry, or afraid, to resume the continuing riddle of their lives. Intimacy was as strange to most of them as the man who brought it. How oddly He spoke.

In Christ, our intimate God, Eden in sandaled feet, Amen

May you not fear the nakedness love will request of you. May it come back to you, like something remembered, something deeply human, a thing profoundly your own.

Your will be done on earth as it is in heaven.
  —Matthew 6:10 NKJV

Love is the complete and demystified will of God. It's not the rehearsal, nor is it the opening act. It's the thing itself. Does it have to be any more complicated than that? It's life out of the tangles, love without the complications, love no less than the vision of life, man fully himself, heaven and earth losing their distinctions, Christianity finding itself, present and eager divinity establishing a realm.

> **In Christ,** *this warm heaven in me,*
> *the love I was made for,* **Amen**

May love abide as overseer, bishop of your little life.

AND IF YOU SPEAK

"A new commandment I give to you, that you love one another; as I have loved you, that you also love one another. By this all will know that you are My disciples, if you have love for one another."
—John 13:34-35 NKJV

And if you speak to me, speak to me with invitation, with that benediction in you that my soul profits by. Speak to me in the language of miracle and mystery, in the language of love, that warms me, that liberates the very God in me, that shelters me within a charity of speech. Speak to me as one in love for the first time, whose happy heart cannot be hushed, whose flame cannot be repressed, smothered, nor ruled by the indifference or the smallness in others. Speak to me of what cannot be explained and yet is so impossibly clear, so godlike and so divine within you. May He expand in you. May He overflow in you, to an uncontainable and living excess that I may gain Him through you, a mutual beneficence.

In Christ, the good profit, Amen

May love be your preference in a world of too many choices.

So Now What? (Graduation)

*"Behold, I send you out as sheep in the midst of wolves:
  be ye therefore wise as serpents, and harmless as doves."*
  —*Matthew 10:16 KJV*

It's a question we've all asked ourselves at one time or another.
We come to some new threshold, an elevation, another
degree, another stone beneath our feet, some finishing place,
an end to some novitiate, a graduating time. We stand alone
at the door of entry into the great experiment. So now what?
What will my acts prove me to be? The fearless entrepreneur?
The careful investor? The fawning obedient? The priest?
The brave soldier? The healer? The drone bee, indentured
to the clock and the buzzing hours? A real person, some
lovely blend of divinity and complication? Or will the years
reveal but a showman, a hollow man, an act to be polished
and groomed, a storefront to be imagined, raised and held
together by words and perceptions, by the grand fiction, the
mere dream of life?

In Christ, the self I seek in me, Amen

In these blind days, may you know the redemption of
true sight.

So Now What? A Prayer

Your ears shall hear a word behind you, saying, "This is the way, walk in it," Whenever you turn to the right hand or whenever you turn to the left.—Isaiah 30:21 NKJV

O, Most Reliable God, True Heart, I would move forward, but my feet are heavy with hesitations. I am locked, anchored, moored deeply in my own misgivings. Give me eyes and sense. Give me a mirror that I may see myself. Give me the sureties that only You can and the wisdom that follows closely by. O, that I may love and get it right, that in loving, life happens. That in love, all things unfold as they were meant, that my life has value, win or lose in the market places, that my trophies sit not upon proud shelves, but in the quiet of the heart and among the shining stars that sparkle in the eye of the Father. That in loving, all conditions are met, all contracts are fulfilled, all debts quieted. For this ascent, give me wings and take from my timid soul the fear of flying.

**In Christ, my Way in this world,
the counsel by which I proceed, Amen**

May you be so centered, so immersed, so consumed, so taken with Him Who confers His gifts upon you that you hardly notice them in operation.

JUNE

Christ, when heaven could keep
"I love you" silent no longer

LET THE SUN HAVE ITS WAY

JUNE 1

Whom have I in heaven but You? And there is none upon earth that I desire besides You.—Psalms 73:25 NKJV

It seems indifferent, as if it doesn't feel what I feel and doesn't care. I despise its light as it creeps upon our hills, its warmth as it steals upon our bed. It is a grey and overcast morning within me, and yet this bright and smiling sun does not agree. Though I am wearied and unsettled, though my bed is nettles and briers, You are the prayer in me that heaven will hear. You are the request in me that will not go unanswered. You are the love that will not be shaken from me. Return to me the hope that I seemed to have talked from myself, the calm that I have fretted away. Peace is Yours alone to give. It rallies at Your command. And let the sun have its way. Let it be warm and welcomed in my skies again. He was right all along.

In Jesus,** the sun smiling at its height, gently mocking at my despair, dispersing it like a mist, **Amen

May Christ be the sun in your happy skies, your Savior at morning, noon, and midnight.

I am the LORD your God, Who teaches you teaches you what is best for you, Who directs you in the way you should go.
  —Isaiah 48:17 NIV

It's a song I wrote for my son's wedding. Young and in love, innocent before the world, it's an affirmation, a promise to assure them, though the way before them is unfamiliar, the distances untried and undetermined, though uncertainty is something they can be certain of, love can be trusted. That love, like a destination fixed between them, brought them this far and only love has the stuff to see them through, a thing settled long before they came to this altar. And like them, we too can put our whole trust in this one bright and unmoving star, the one plotted on our inward charts, the one that puts stillness into the compass where the heart seeks its way, the one that lights our passage homeward, heaven's radiant jewel, even Him, *Him Who laid this path before us, Who promised we could go from here without a care, and not be afraid of the mystery, 'Cause love will get us there.*

In Christ, the destination fixed between us, **Amen**

When the years have passed and you begin to look back on all the things that at this moment may seem a bit unclear, may you know that it was more than just good fortune, that *it was love that brought you here.*

GOODNESS: FIRST AMONG THE MANY SPOILS OF THE DAY

JUNE 3

How great is your goodness that you have stored up for those who fear you, that you have given to those who trust you. You do this for all to see.—Psalms 31:19 NCV

May this day show such benevolence to you, such high measures of blessedness, such pure excesses of joy, that you may know above all mere suspicions that heaven is friendly and that somebody's paying attention! May the goodness of the Lord be first among the many spoils this day brings to you. May you recognize it when it comes to you and in whatever form it comes.

In Christ, when heaven could keep 'I love you'
silent no longer, Amen

May blessedness ornament your day, glittering upon you, like a suit well fitted, shining brighter than heaven breaking into smiles.

It Wouldn't Happen in Our Time

And they continued steadfastly in the apostles' doctrine and fellowship, in the breaking of bread, and in prayers. Then fear came upon every soul, and many wonders and signs were done through the apostles. Now all who believed were together, and had all things in common.
—*Acts 2:42-44 NKJV*

They were food for lions and for the dark entertainments of the Caesars. Desperation imposed itself upon them in swift running tides. It distilled into the blood, writing itself deep into their code of life. It mingled together with love to give them a beginning, a beginning that could have only happened in such a time, when every hour and every minute was precious. It sifted the heart of debris. It made love authentic, immediate, relevant. They knew heaven was close, one step, one martyrdom away. Love bound them together, love that was larger than their disputes or differences. It was currency among them, the gold by which they traded among themselves, the coin that purchased heaven. *The birth of Christianity would not have happened in a world like our own.*

In Christ, the love that gave us our beginnings, Christ, our genesis and our exodus, Christ, the first of blood, prince of martyrs, Amen

May love act as a bridge, as a translator, a link, a mediator, as sovereign over the very least of your exchanges.

VEILS

JUNE 5

Nevertheless, when one turns to the Lord, the veil is taken away.
  —2 Corinthians 3:16 NKJV

In fear of discovery, we tend to hide our faces or some
inglorious feature, and we offer something else to the world,
something less, a fiction, a mere resemblance. But there is
enough mystery in humanity already and in our exchanges
with each other without that which we invent ourselves.
*O, how little we know who we are! And yet, how we long to engage
with life, with others as hungry for love and warmth as ourselves.
How little we dare the risk love requests of us. Truth hides itself
within our veils and we think ourselves safe, hidden, all the time
fearing the wilderness of knowing.*

In Christ, what love will ask of me, Amen

Veils. May you have little need of them. May the glory of love
be too bright, too jealous, too violent in opposition to them.
May love divest you of them, liberating you, as your body,
His present temple, has no use of them. May Christ be all the
covering you need. May you be clothed with Him alone.

To Be or Not To Be?

Consider the lilies, how they grow: they neither toil nor spin; and yet I say to you, even Solomon in all his glory was not arrayed like one of these.—Luke 12:27 NKJV

My first request in prayer usually sounds like this: *HELP!* or *FORGIVE ME, LORD!* But today was different. I actually heard myself say that I simply desire *to be,* that the work would be taken out of being who I am, that I may mimic God in His being, to walk about in that kind of freedom, even as He Who is THE EXISTING ONE, THE ONE WHO IS (Jehovah), with no disguises, no veils, with no fictions or myths to explain me to the world, with no law, no boundaries, no government in me but love. To live by the higher inclination within me, to be led by a divine inner compass, trusting heaven itself to be the true and fixed North of this day's adventures in simply being me.

In Christ, *the joy of being who I am,* **Amen**

May *being* take precedence over *doing.* It is the verb of love. *I AM THAT I AM* is how He explained himself to Moses.

JUNE 7

For out of the abundance of the heart the mouth speaks.
  —*Matthew 12:34 NKJV*

When something beautiful and mysterious is happening to the soul, when it is overcome with warmth, it will express itself in speech that is elevated, waking miracle and majesty in little medleys of language, setting the plainness of life and the moment to a score of music. *The heart tells its secrets in lyric, for love must sing or be silent.* I suspect the early church knew this because of the hymns they sang and the scripture they chanted. The Bible itself is just one big lyric, perfect and finely tuned with mystery, truth, beauty, ecstasy, divinity, proportion, and all the elements that love is known by.

In Christ, *the muse and the theme of life,* **Amen**

May your words come even as Christ came, as divinity dressed in servants' raiment.

LOVE IN ITS OWN WORDS—A PRAYER

These things we also speak, not in words which man's wisdom teaches but which the Holy Spirit teaches, comparing spiritual things with spiritual.—1 Corinthians 2:13 NKJV

Call forth from the thickets, from the deep tangle of my heart, that which is Your own, Lord, that which may be shy or silenced altogether in my denials and refusals of love. That love may loose itself in its native beauty, in a celebration of speech. That my soul may sing as it was made to, as heaven designed it, to its own peculiar detail and lyric. Turn the plainness of my life to poetry. I will trust heaven with that which only heaven can do.

In Christ, my life set to a score, my plainness set to poetry, Amen

Before the engines of the working day begin to whine, before the first wheel turns, may heaven fill you with today's first flowing measures of gladness.

JUNE 9

"...For they all put in out of their abundance, but she out of her poverty put in all that she had, her whole livelihood."
—*Mark 12:44 NKJV*

"You preach like a desperate man!" I remember telling him afterwards. It had the strangeness and the shock of something genuine and by an authority that gave him speech and fire, that was naked in him, unscripted and untaught, that drew me into his circle of flames as he spoke. There was no net beneath him. It wasn't verbal pyrotechnics, charisma, nor any of the usual ornaments of Christian pulpiteers. But I knew somehow that it had everything to do with love. I'm not sure what happened to the man, but I do remember what excitement I felt in my soul, what closeness I felt to the mystery, and to the God he spoke of. I knew I had been aroused from some unknown slumber.

In Christ, *what love and the desperate preach*, **Amen**

May others recognize in you what they long for in themselves.

LOVE AND THE LAST BITE
KIND OF GOOD

...If you find my beloved...tell him I am lovesick!
—Song of Solomon 5:8 NKJV

You've just scoffed down almost all of a really great sandwich,
or some dreamy piece of chocolate that seemed to linger
with little spasms in your mouth as it melted away, or it's ice
cream so thick with ooze and suspended bits of Butterfinger®,
Heath Bar®, Reeses®, etc. that you bypass the ceremony of a
bowl altogether and eat it right out of its frosty little carton.
You know what I mean, it's all yours. There's a carnival in
the mouth. And the kid is loose again. Then you're down to
the last bite. You stare at it. You meditate. You brood over it.
You prepare the attack in your mind. You're focused. You're
in that zone, that little hesitation just before the finish. There
is but a brief distance between you and ecstasy. You don't
remember the other bites being quite this good. The wait
itself is pleasurable and intolerable at the same time.

In Christ, the joy in the wait, love with all the toppings, Amen

May love always be that last bite kind of good.

FOOL

Let no one deceive himself. If anyone among you seems to be wise in this age, let him become a fool that he may become wise.
—*1 Corinthians 3:18 NKJV*

Christ is as close as we may come to understanding love. He is all the explanation we are given. Still, it is difficult. Christ is not easy. And we have busied ourselves with other things in retreat. *I feel so foolish in the evaluation of things, Lord. We do not understand eternity, though it moves so freely about us. We do not understand the love that framed the heavens, that stacked our bones, that greased our joints, and hid something divine in the circuits of our blood. But Lord, receive my thankfulness, this crude offering from my lips, this testament from a grateful and yet inarticulate man. I am love's fool. But I am love's. And that is something. Maybe I am no fool at all.*

In Christ, *Who takes speech from me, like the glory of morning stealing over a hill, Amen*

May the glory resident within you be extroverted, outwardly mobile, upwardly poised, nice to its neighbors, liberal with itself. May it bound in eager strides upon your plots of earth like the Almighty chambered within it.

To Play, to Drift, To Be Wooed by Majesty

Honour and majesty are before him: strength and beauty are in his sanctuary.—Psalms 96:6 KJV

Lord, let me enter into Your sanctuary this day as a child, unburdened with Self, free to play, to drift, to be wooed by majesty. Let me not toil in hearing or recoil at things I do not understand. Let each word, each syllable in step with the next keep its appointment in me today. I listen as a novice, as one under study. I listen as the desperate to a word of relief. I listen as a lover listens to music and suffers deep pangs in the heart. That I may see new things and consider the old way, even what I believed yesterday as but a passing dream, to be forgotten among forgotten things, or to be reordered even as my life. Unsettle my beliefs. They are nothing. My opinion is nothing. My agenda is nothing. They are millstones and not jewels about my neck. I am alive with expecting. I am youth before You.

In Christ, the distance between me and my truest self, Amen

May any sense of regret or loss be confounded by inspiration, by a new vision of life, a new hope, and may it have the strength of wonder, of things redeemed from a more innocent age.

Uncertainty. It's Not Such an Ugly Word.

June 13

"Eye has not seen, nor ear heard, nor have entered into the heart of man the things which God has prepared for those who love Him." But God has revealed them to us through His Spirit. For the Spirit searches all things, yes, the deep things of God.
—*1 Corinthians 2:9-10 NKJV*

I live, O Lord, with mystery, with uncertainty, with Your hiddenness. In wisdom, You keep those secrets that are forbidden to me, that are too high for me. You make me trust when there is no sense of You. I am overwhelmed most of the time and faith must answer when reason and my senses are mute. You ask me to find comfort in my own blindness, to tread a path I cannot see before me, to follow the footsteps of an invisible God, to make this uncertainty my very way, and to pioneer my little life by a hope that You have set before me by such a peculiar and yet beautiful light.

In Christ, my uncertainty, my sure God, Amen

May you trust when there is no sense of Him.

…Casting down arguments and every high thing that exalts itself against the knowledge of God, bringing every thought into captivity to the obedience of Christ… —2 Corinthians 10:5 NKJV

May the argument within you die. May your soul concern itself with better things. May all layers of it be exposed and vulnerable, till it be wasted by the higher elements in you, till it wither beneath the bright sun of mercy, reconciliation, forgiveness, charity, and selflessness. *Cast off the very name of Christianity if you must, that you may be the Christian you are commanded to be,* within whom argument is pale, forgotten, and dead, for whom you lead a martyr's life. And when argument dies, what is left? Only love. Therefore, let us cast off what is human, welcome what is divine.

**In Christo, the end of argument, the name
love speaks in its place, Amen**

May the goodness of God be so rich, so bountiful, so generous, so loving and so large, even you can't shoo it away or lose it to an argument.

More YES

Oh, taste and see that the LORD is good; Blessed is the man who trusts in Him!—Psalms 34:8 NKJV

Lord, how my world is transformed in a single word! How I am made glad in affirmations, in heaven's prolific and agreeable Yes, alive with repetitions, profuse, teeming with light, mystery, and gift-giving promise! It spreads over me with wings that carry me from myself, deep into each amazing day that I may claim as my own. Tomorrow will come, though I need not speak of it now. It will not concern me till it need to, till it be here, till the sun returns if God so chooses, till I may call it today. Till then, it is the tomorrow that I think not of. Grant me Yes. Confer it upon me, Lord. Establish it firmly in the chronicle of all my hopeful days. Yes, God. Yes. Yes, O Christ. Take Yes from me and give it sweetly back again. And again.

**In Christ, when I searched heaven itself
for the appropriate Word, Amen**

May love be your lexicon when a word is needed, your '3 down' or your '7 across' when there are too many blank spaces. May it be your common book of prayer when petition or necessity would press heaven for an answer.

JUNE 16

…Soon…—Revelation 3:11, 22:7, 22:12, 22:20 NCV

It shouldn't just be the privilege of the desperate or those alone who know their days are short, for the remaining moments of life to be lived at an altered pitch, for the heart to jettison useless and irrelevant baggage, discarding what is unneccessary, the surplus weights and excesses, refining priorities. *O, that we could love enough to be this present, this current, this immediate, this deliberate in action, this relevant in speech, this transparent in thought and in the warm gifting of the self, as if there were no tomorrow. That we could say today what needs to be said at last, having no tomorrow to put it off. To give someone we love what is ours to give them, and to give it now. Now, where love is always at its best.*

In Christ, *love present, love current, love immediate,* **Amen**

May wonder, anticipation, and suspense keep youth captive in the blood.

IN THE MYSTS OF EDEN

JUNE 17

Then the LORD God called to Adam and said to him, "Where are you?"—Genesis 3:9 NKJV

In Eden, God was not so hidden. Heaven was not so distant. There existed an intimacy, a nakedness between God and man, an innocence the soul loves. Little did man think about where humanity ended or divinity began, where the border lay between heaven and earth. God was sufficient. Faith and hope were the provisions God gave to first man upon his banishment, like twin guides that would help him find his way home again. *Love was the journey. Faith and hope were but the lamps.* And yet there was something necessary and inevitable in it all, like a law at work, like redemption taking its first steps, something crimson at the root of the tree, and a figure unnoticed, stirring, shrouded in the mysts of Eden.

In Christ, the path home, Amen

May your soul be a house of light and divinity, a place of counsel, a place of quiet, a refuge in an uneasy time.

O Lord, open my lips, and my mouth shall show forth Your praise.
—Psalms 51:15 NKJV

Christ, the shape my words take as my soul rises in petition.
Christ, the stillness that comes over me. Christ, the hub and sweet
center of life, my earth in its place, my planets ordered and dispersed,
set in orbits around this bright and inconquerable Sun. Christ, my
joy that has no fences. Christ, my deep fire, like pent-up youth, Eden
remembered in the currents of my blood. Christ, at the setting of my
sun, the day now weeping soft epitaph at the dying of the light.
Christ and the night that quiets me, my prayer's long pilgrimage
ended, hushed at its last notes of Amen. And Christ, until the Sun
again. O, You strange God, You strange and beautiful God.

In Christ, the one and lovely, strange and beautiful, Amen

May petition and praise within you give way to something
warmer, something deeper, greater than the common forms
and habits of devotion. For in this odd affliction, words are
no longer sufficient. They no longer serve as useful currency.
There is only essence joined with essence, by mystery and by
mutual assent.

To Be a Lover

Therefore be imitators of God as dear children.—Ephesians 5:1 NKJV

…And drink; yes, drink deeply, lovers.—Song of Solomon 5:1 NCV

To be a lover is to be like Him Who is love. To be a lover is to live by the one command He gave us, to love as He loved, to spend ourselves at love's slightest request, to be invisible as He is invisible, to be hidden as in the majesty of love's simplest of acts. A lover's life is a surrendered life. It's a total giving over of self, a reinterpretation of life by way of love. All who are called by this name have their genesis, their primal connective cord, their umbilicus in Him, in Christ, Who is everything to the lover's soul, code, canon, and creed.

In Christ, code, canon, and creed, Amen

May the God of Glory find a place of rest in you. May the Son of Man have a place to lay His head at last. May the Law you honor, honor you.

LOVER'S CATECHISM:
LOVERS FORGIVE

A lover's prayer: *Our Father which art in heaven, Hallowed be thy name. Thy kingdom come. Thy will be done in earth, as it is in heaven. Give us this day our daily bread. And forgive us our debts, as we forgive our debtors. And lead us not into temptation, but deliver us from evil: For thine is the kingdom, and the power, and the glory, forever. Amen.*—Matthew 6:9-13 KJV

Forgiveness in any form is a prayer that settles in beauty upon the ear of God, like poetry, like music that pleases Him. With three lovely words, *I forgive you,* we unbolt heavy doors, we spring the hidden locks, and we invite heaven between us. Freedom is as simple as a word and LOVERS are the true poets among us, the seasoned wordsmiths. LOVERS live lives of reconciliation and release, who call back an angry or misunderstood time and redeem it, who wash offenders in warm and generous fonts of light, selfless and tender, and seat love upon the conqueror's seat. Mercy is a song ever humming about in LOVERS' heads.

In Christ, the Word itself, the Poetmaker's son, Amen

May the language of forgiveness come easy to you, as one's own native tongue, remembering heaven is your homeland, the merciful country.

LOVER'S CATECHISM:
LOVERS HAVE FEELINGS TOO

JUNE 21

"Be angry, and do not sin": do not let the sun go down on your wrath…—Ephesians 4:26-27 NKJV

A LOVER is free to feel what they feel, from the comic to the tragic, and all dramatic intensities in between. They are free to burn when angry, to ignite when fire and outrage heat the blood, to feel joy, grief, despair, bitterness, to feel wounded, hurt, afraid, to be happy, ecstatic, hopeful. They can be detached, proud, that is, until love, till order and rule take precedence, till body and soul are hushed by the voice of authority within them. Till Him. For there is too much Christ there for the emotions to go unchecked and sabotage the soul. LOVERS catch themselves. *And love always does the right thing. Even when it does the wrong thing. It cannot fail. Love is the great medicine of the earth and LOVERS are the medicine men, the healers, whose God is always before them, and at their disposal.*

**In Jesus, our passionate Christ, the God
not afraid to feel, Amen**

May love overrule feelings. May the passions lose their authority. May love be the parent to their child.

LOVER'S CATECHISM:
LOVERS, WELL, THEY LOVE

Arise, shine; for your light has come! And the glory of the LORD is risen upon you.—Isaiah 60:1 NKJV

There is nothing, nothing, nothing, quite like that moment when love awakens the heart. And there is no going back to the way things were before. All things are different. By some overthrow, some change of government, we are banished from the life we had previously known just a moment, just a lifetime before. All things are changed and in an instant, in an unsuspecting time. It is the LOVER alone, the happy fortunate, who is truly awake on this sleepy planet.

In Christ, my new world, Amen

May this large life in you be companioned with generosity, with humility, meekness, kindness, gentleness, and the responsibility that accompanies true greatness.

THE EYE OF THE STORM:
A DIFFERENT VIEW

JUNE 23

Then they cry out to the LORD in their trouble, and He brings them out of their distresses. He calms the storm, so that its waves are still. Then they are glad because they are quiet; so He guides them to their desired haven.—Psalms 107:28-30 NKJV

Peter came to himself at last and began to see as for the first time. His was now a different world. His violent weeping[8] washed him of his misbelief, even as it cleansed him of his former self. He was reborn in the midst of a storm, awakened by thunder pent up in him. For many of us, it's in just such a place that sight is finally made possible, when all the illusions, all the myths and mirages, when all the usual props and supports of a fragile and invented faith can no longer stand the blast. *Think of the change that came over Jonah. Or the transformation of the Magdalene that made her name beautiful among the Marys. And the man of the tombs, clothed and in his right mind.*

In Christ, my calm in the midst of things, Amen

May love hold firmly against all brooding elements, against the intrigues of the small and the loveless, against the cunning of words, charms, and other secret arts, against excess, against neglect and want, against all lesser lights, against the voices of all the minor prophets of this world and against the unbelief of an entire generation.

8 *Luke 22:61-62*

BY ANOTHER NAME

And I will write on him My new name.—Revelation 3:12 NKJV

Though I was given a name at birth and though that name separates me out in a world dizzy with names, and though I've learned at last to be comfortable with that name, even as it signs all my checks and fills out all my forms, there is a another name I carry within me, a greater, truer name, a name I do not yet know, a name You keep to Yourself, a name I will be recognized by in its time, that shapes me even now and determines who I am. O Tender Christ, even as marriage changes names and the order of lives, take me into Your house, even as one betrothed, as one promised, a child, a brother, a friend. Let me love till love confers upon me my true and inevitable name, the one too deep in me now, the one I have no language to articulate, no song yet to draw it forth.

In Christ, First Name in the household of love, Amen

May your name and the life associated with it be joyful in the mouth of God, established firm in the index of things sacred to Him.

The Geometry of Love

'He drew a circle that shut me out, A heretic, a rebel, a thing to flout. But love and I had the wit to win; We drew a circle that took him in.'
—From Edwin Markham, American poet (1852-1940)

In spite of its age and of having suffered too many misquotes, it's still so beautifully Christian, the essence of a higher faith, a more genuine faith. Love that transcends my inward politics. Love, bigger than my vision of life, more invasive than pain, longer than money or blood. I am commanded to love that large, to make my circle of love pliable, penetrable, elastic, permeable, roomy and round. With each argument I sustain within myself, with each petty refusal or denial of love, each time I hoard my true gold, my circle begins to close in on me till little room is left, except for one. And what should be a sanctuary, sufficient with light and warmth, becomes a lonely prison. *Let them in!*

In Christ, my theory of government, Amen

May your faith be big enough to embrace those who believe differently than you. May your heart be heavy with them. May love take you to the extremes and excesses you never could have imagined of yourself. And may it take from you the sharp edges, the abrupt turns, and all opposing geometries.

SOMETHING IN COMMON

Therefore if there is any consolation in Christ, if any comfort of love, if any fellowship of the Spirit, if any affection and mercy, fulfill my joy by being like-minded, having the same love, being of one accord, of one mind.—Philippians 2:1-2 NKJV

Love is the most common of all common elements that thrive deep in the heart of man and yet it is the alien, the outcast, the stranger that wanders about the earth, the Christ that the world heaps its hostilities upon. Love is still the root and spring. And though the surfaces have long cooled, it remains the common core, the heated center of all things human. It's inescapable. It's in the air, in the water supply. Love endows even the dullest of our days with something sacred. It puts the sacred back into the general currents of life and gives me renewed kinship with all mankind, past, present, and future. *O Love, awaken the soul of the great congregation! Rouse the earth itself! Crowd hopeful Man into that grand and royal fellowship of his origins!*

In Christ, where the soul of earth is tending, Amen

May this big world shrink and become smaller in the eye of love. May *possibility* have a new presence among your meditations. May words like *global* and *international* find a place of prominence in your vocabulary.

Until Faith and
Until She Came Along

June 27

By faith we understand that the worlds were framed by the word of God, so that the things which are seen were not made of things which are visible.—Hebrews 11:3 NKJV

I had not been faithful to anyone. It was a bad habit. I never really thought about it. Or cared. But that was then. A life ago. This is now, after years of surrender. Christ was the start, the turnstile, my school, my boarding place. I had, from childhood, acquired the skill of engagement but with my motor humming, to engage and yet be fully in control, to be in and to be out at the same time. I learned the great secret of being in a constant state of preflight. There was no faith in me, except in the mutability of all things, in the inconstancy and in the brevity of relationships. There was no faith in me except for the knowledge that all things change rapidly, that at best you are alone. I had created and lived within the great fiction of my life, that I was not faithful, nor capable of being faithful to anyone. Until Christ. Until faith. And until she came along.

In Christ, this big life and the faith to live it, Amen

May faith come easier than you suspect, the step and not the leap.

IT JUST DOESN'T GET
ANY BETTER THAN THIS!

But it doesn't matter. The important thing is that in every way, whether for right or wrong reasons, they are preaching about Christ. So I am happy, and I will continue to be happy.—Philippians 1:18 NCV

You're at a ball game. Baseball (it's June). It's deeply American. I suspect that printed in the dust of our past are traces of cleat marks. It's late afternoon. There's still sun left, but the heat has gone from it. It's cool in every way cool can be cool. It just doesn't get any better than this! There are no demands. Life is humming and as lazy as late summer days are supposed to be. Time to groove. You're not there to think. You may not even be there for the game. Maybe you're there for the diversion that baseball, like no other event, can be. You're there to loose the restraints, to yell, to laugh, to sing silly songs, to eat hazardous food, to call back the kid. Life as we once dreamed it. But then you see it, as you always see it at stadiums everywhere, or scrawled on bathroom walls, on buses, overpasses, or bumper stickers. It's long been part of the sports tradition, an accepted part of Americana. *JOHN 3:16.* Okay. Maybe it's not your way. But find your own. *Gospel your world! Jesus someone around you today!*

In Christ, *the gospel the world wants of me,* **Amen**

Where love plays, may you be the child again.

SIRS, WHAT MUST I DO TO BE SAVED?

JUNE 29

Then he called for a light, ran in, and fell down trembling before Paul and Silas. And he brought them out and said, "Sirs, what must I do to be saved?"—Acts 16:29-30 NKJV

Love is the one true thing, the one redeeming thing upon which the salvation of the world depends, a salvation that is not gained by convincing anyone of anything or by promoting an agenda. Our invitations must be deeper than that and engage with life below its common surfaces, where only humility can unlock the code. I am to be no less than love made visible on the earth, an earth so wanting of its warmth and light, so needful of its divinity. *This is the Christianity that the world is looking for, the Christianity that makes the heavens themselves tremble with joy and celebration.*

In Christ, the redeemer in me, love in flesh and visible, **Amen**

When the world itself asks, *"Sirs, what must I do to be saved?"* may love be your response. Practice global warming. Practice local warming. Mimic God. John 3:16 your world.

No Fear

There is no fear in love; but perfect love casts out fear, because fear involves torment. But he who fears has not been made perfect in love.—1 John 4:18 NKJV

Early man needed more direct parenting, so God showed Himself in ways which we are not accustomed. The world is all grown up now. At least this is what it tells itself. But as for me, my fears seem to have intelligence, a convincing one, and because I fear, my love is not perfect. I am an impediment to myself. I need love on autopilot, to operate independent of me, to parent my child. I need love to be a shield when I am threatened, paralyzed, or mute with alarm. I need love to *cast me out of me,* that I may follow a path of selflessness, of otherness, a path so divine, and yet so deeply human. I need the assurances that only love can give me, as I need the God at the heart of them. *Love is perfect. It's me who lags.*

In Christ, this perfect love, Amen

May Christ be your confidence, your eyes in darkness, your hands when you cannot feel, your heart when its paces are unsure, the word in your mouth when fear, like a thief, steals your tongue.

JULY

Christ, the faith it takes to love

THE UNDISCOVER'D COUNTRY

"Did not our heart burn within us while He talked with us on the road, and while He opened the Scriptures to us?"
  —Luke 24:32 NKJV

It's early. I'm lying next to my wife and the room is quiet but for the faint sound of breathing. She dreams often. And though she may tell me her dreams I am still no more than a stranger to them. It's mystery that keeps love kindled beneath the warm covers of morning. Shakespeare called death the *undiscover'd country,* but I think perhaps the real *undiscover'd country* may just be my brother or my sister, my neighbor, my wife, my child, myself. Subtract mystery from love, subtract the unknown and we must call love by another name. *I search in hope of you.* The you wherein my true reflection hides itself. *O, how vast is the human heart, and how unknown! I am but a new Columbus on a Sea of Darkness. Love, the brave and lonely passage.*

In Christ, my fare paid, the wine dark sea before me, Amen

May you celebrate the mystery of life, that which reason must exchange for faith. May it add a measure of joyful suspense to each day.

JULY 2

...And a fool's voice is known by his many words.
  —*Ecclesiastes 5:3 NKJV*

In love, words are insufficient. It's the difference between the mere image or idea of God and the living presence of Him, of that which may be contained within a house of words and that which cannot. *Still, I'm always hopeful, always on alert for that happy accident, that spillage in my lab that changes everything, that one true sentence, that link of words charged with ecstatic electricity, divinity, and brave innocence, that hums with that certain frequency, all in the hope that love may find its way in a world of spin and make-believe. That's something, I suppose. But then I think, "Who am I that I dare open my mouth?" I am but a jester in the court of Majesty, the Prince of Wails.*

In Jesus, my sufficient Christ, the one clear Word, Amen

May blessedness echo upon you who dare to speak and to act in love's behalf, who give wings to the God inside you.

E Pluribus Unum[9]—A Prayer

Now you are the body of Christ, and members individually.
—1 Corinthians 12:27 NKJV

Let LOVE, shut up like rivers, be loosed in flood tides over us. Let it come in tempest, Lord, till we are carried helpless upon its currents, till we are broken beneath its wake, till we become a people and not the shadow of a people, till we love and not waste ourselves on what is not love, on meaningless and unprofitable pursuit, till we no longer find pride in our divisions, till we are come to our senses at last, till by some act of love's sovereignty we are fully ourselves again, till we conform to the glory of our original design, with no agenda but love, having no opinion but Christ, no name but His, no citizenship but what heaven confers upon us.

In Jesus, the good medicine between me and my brother, Amen

Even as we fear God, may we so fear the power of love, the fear synonymous with awe and wonder, dread and reverence, till all life becomes sacred, till we see Christ in the lowliest among us.

---

9 *e pluribus unum – out of the many, one*

HE SERVES HIS COUNTRY BEST
WHOSE GOD IS FIRST

JULY 4

*Live as free people, but do not use your freedom as an excuse
to do evil. Live as servants of God.*—1 Peter 2:16 NCV

*Lord, I surrender the things which govern me, from the outermost
to the centermost of me: my voice in the congress of life, my place in
the fellowship of Man, my convictions, my belief, my agenda. I am
no longer my own. And if I rise up, if I assert myself in the great
theatres of life, in the arenas where ideas come together, in the
debating places where opinions gather and brood, in harmony or in
havoc, in concord or chaos, be my judgment, my good opinion in all
things, that in a day of decision, I would be Yours, a man of God,
a man at peace with his own soul, a man that has no earth, no
allegiance, no country but Christ Himself. In this I do my neighbor,
my homeland, and the America of my blood, the greatest good.*

In Christ, the greatest good in me to do, Amen

May love hold the hidden scales to all your judgments, to all
questionable measures.

HOLINESS: WHERE LOVE
FEELS AT HOME

But be holy in all you do, just as God, the One who called you, is holy.—*1 Peter 1:15 NCV*

May holiness thrive in the common rites and habits of your day, holiness that puts life in harness, holiness that is easily recognized, that is irresistible, sovereign, dependable, holiness that makes a healer of you, holiness that does not offend or alienate in its highness, holiness that is gentle, that puts tenderness back into the touch, back into the nature of man, holiness that is responsible, whose foundation, whose center of gravity is love, holiness that reflects Him alone Who is love, Who desires continual presence in the mind, the heart, and among the higher senses, as one looking for a home.

In Christ, where love feels at home, Amen

May the peace of God settle deep within your walls and in the foundations of your house. May it wrestle the wind to whispers, silence a howling and accusing earth before she cries out.

JULY 6

For I think that God has displayed us, the apostles, last, as men condemned to death; for we have been made a spectacle to the world, both to angels and to men. —1 Corinthians 4:9 NKJV

There is a God Who unsettles me, that overthrows my plans, my confidences, Who distracts me in my dreaming, a God Who troubles me, like a maddening pulse, like joy electric—hidden in the courses of my blood. I cannot contain Him nor can I quiet Him. *O Wondrous God, Who posts these fences that border me, Who establishes my limits, Who shelters me in His pavilions, Who architects the frame and foundation upon which my little house is built, may I never deny You, but if I should, if I should consent to some renegade passion or some hidden mutiny in me, O remain, remain the God seated in my heart's core.*

In Christ, *my unsettling, my lovely undoing,*
my rearranging, **Amen**

May you love enough in this life to hurt for it.

THAT WHICH MADE HIM KING

My heart was hot within me; While I was musing, the fire burned.
  —Psalms 39:3 NKJV

*Lord, grant me that which made David king. Penitence and
poetry that labored together to find a common solution to his pain.
Thankfulness that could not help but sing. Humility that mixed
with Majesty, a rare thing in kings. Madness that stripped him of
his robes and his titles, to celebrate the Zion of his joy, wild and
naked in him. Love that governed him, a sovereign over sovereigns.
And most of all, an awareness of You that gave him words, words
that shaped the mouth of prayer, that put petition and praise in the
tongues of multitudes after him. My words stumble in my mouth
this morning. They chatter like flames, unordered, and ungovernable,
stronger than my patience, more prevailing than my well-arranged
ideas of things. And yet now I think, with the overthrow of civility
and reason in this one complaint, how strange that this prayer is the
very answer I sought, that it would ravel out the David shut up in
my bones.*

Uncontrollably, irrefutably, irrevocably in love, Amen

As it was with David, may God love to watch you dance, to
be your absolute and unguarded self.

YOU BELONG TO ME!
A BENEDICTION

"I have called you by name, and you are Mine."—Isaiah 43:1 NCV

May doubt go on holiday. May it lose all maps, all passages back to you. If it looks at you with the longing of an old love, may it see nothing, no reflection in the living glass no warmth, no suggestion of its own form. May fear rule in another world, having found no loyal subject in your own. May worry have no voice, no good arguments to sell. May sorrow lose its familiar way. May bitterness die a death too deep for waking at all, missing its appointment with you altogether. And if love surfaces in the absence of those former tenants, if it seeks you out, may it find no resistance in you, nothing to slow its progress. May love have its way with you, even as the conqueror to a vanquished city. *"You belong to me!" it says, with a voice that seems to thunder from the mouth of God.*

**In Jesus, my conquering Christ, the voice
that thunders over me, Amen**

May joy have authority over your tongue, over all things that busy themselves in the mind, over the many transactions with life as it gathers about you.

JULY 9

You are the light of the world.—Matthew 5:14 NKJV

May you shine bright today, within your own circles and outside them, on that moving million-footed pavement where life gathers and hums, wherever love has appointments today. Illumine your world. Be submissive and watching, innocent and courageous. And may love in you be so evolved, so articulate, so at home, so practiced, so easy, so weightless, so clear and so accessible that others may warm themselves in its illuminating and inviting glow.

In Christ, at the intersection of Light and Life, Amen

May the world around you today be benevolent with light. May Christ be the bright and deathless filament to your happy little bulb.

WHO SAID LOVE WAS EASY?

JULY 10

Now may the Lord direct your hearts into the love of God and into the patience of Christ.—2 Thessalonians 3:5 NKJV

To consider the needs of others before those of my own. *That's not easy.* To be selfless, invisible, to be the servant love would have me to be. *That's not easy.* To show kindness where none was given or expected. *No, that's not easy.* To do good if it's within my power to do good, though it take something from me, something costly. To forget and never recall an injury. To be surrendered to all that love would ask of me. To put to death my arguments and my options. This is already beginning to sound like way too much work. But it's we who are difficult. *Remember, love is easy. We are the work.*

> ### In Christ, the work that remains,
> ### the work already done, Amen

May your heart be mended by what it heals. May it become full by what it gives away.

WHERE LOVE WAITS

Turn to me and have mercy on me, because I am lonely and hurting.
  —*Psalms 25:16 NCV*

Where love waits, as in a lonely house, where the widow eats
alone in her kitchen, where mornings come unwanted and
bring with them but a sad and empty light that creeps too
silent along the yellow walls, where the forgotten eat their
bread in quiet, where loneliness has no medicine, where the
old man has but memories to people his little room, where
the single mother wearies herself with care, where injustice
finds no resistance, no restraints, where indifference has no
eyes or ears, where sorrow threatens to fatten itself upon the
helpless and the unguarded, may love in you find its duty, its
champion, its friend, its kindness, its vision, its action, its
mirror, its redeemer, its Christ.

In Christ, where love waits, Amen

May holiness set a seal on you, an irrevocable mark of
divinity, of ownership, a living crest that cannot be plagiarized
nor counterfeited, a statute written within the margins of
your one life, a living Gospel set in the fleshy midst of you,
Love with limbs and sense, Love with a fluency of words and
a mouth to put them in. Christ in echo.

LOVER'S CATECHISM:
PAY ATTENTION

God is in the details.—Mies van der Rohe, Architect (1886-1969)

Our denials of love begin mostly at the smallest levels, but the hurt is large. Someone close could be asking, *"Do you see me? Do you hear me? Do you know that I am here? Do you know who I am? Have you looked close enough? Are you glad I am here? Do you not know what I am thinking? Can you not tell me why I weep? Do you not know what makes me laugh? Have you noticed anything different today?"* Love is in the details. Pay attention to them. For love delights in the littleness of things. Great kindnesses live there. Test it as soon as you can.

In Christ, *love's finishing work, heaven's greatest detail,* **Amen**

Love abounds warm with invitation. Expect a crowd. Be yourself. Love is a divine legal agreement. Trust love with the fine print.

They immediately left their nets and followed Him.
  —*Mark 1:18 NKJV*

What if your vision of life was suddenly altered or supplanted somehow for a strange new one? And order as you know it was suddenly reordered, your rule of life given over for something better, higher, something you could not have expected or imagined? *Warning:* Love will confer upon you a new rule, and with it, a new set of scales. You will see and consider new things. You will hear what you could not hear before. Your priorities, your politics, your responses to life, how you invest your soul, your words, your actions—it all changes. Love transforms all your receptors and rewrites all contracts with the earth you inhabit. *And again be warned:* It doesn't come without a price. Love asks nothing but everything. Like heaven itself, love is but a death away, one authentic surrender, one glorious martyrdom from you.

Courageously in love, Amen

May Christ be heaven enough for you.

A Child of This Age—A Prayer

But mark this: There will be terrible times in the last days. People will be lovers of themselves, lovers of money, boastful, proud…
—2 Timothy 3:1-2 NIV

I stumble in my pursuit of You, Lord, for I am yet deeply attached to this odd invention of myself. With all the consent and agreements of this world, I have woven my own god, who, in a certain light, looks like me. A child of this age, I am a true patriot of this Great America of Souls, where Self is religion, where Fashion is sovereign, and Money is the visible god. And I am caught in my own thickets, my own traps and tangles, the sticky web of ME. This prayer is severe, but so is the God to Whom I appeal. Your love is mightier than storms and winds, mightier than the proud kingdoms of this earth, than my folly, than all the seductions of the age and all the bindings of this misdirected world.

In Christ, my disenchantment with this world, my growing pursuit of the next, Amen

May love that has no limits show you the line you dare not cross and give you militant resolve in a world that says such a line doesn't exist.

ECSTASY

Now Hannah spoke in her heart; only her lips moved, but her voice was not heard. Therefore Eli thought she was drunk.
—1 Samuel 1:13 NKJV

Ecstasy is what results when riot and rule come together as they do in love. If you can imagine restrained unrestraint, ordered disorder. Psalms, prophetic acts and utterances have all been kindled, processed in these deep fires of love, fires that do not extinguish themselves, fires that must be vented, as in speech, in acts, in kindnesses, in charity, in the strange events that bring heaven to earth. *Ecstasy is not the uncontrollable wild rampage of the emotions, the heart out of harness, but rather immortality finding itself in us, establishing its rule and expressing itself in a world of misbelievers who just think we're drunk.*

In Christ, *ecstasy in harness,* Amen

When you are faint with love, when the heart is overthrown in sweetness, may He strengthen you as in a day of raisins and apples[10]. May you have appetite for little else.

LONELY IN LOVE

Indeed the hour is coming, yes, has now come, that you will be scattered, each to his own, and will leave Me alone. And yet I am not alone, because the Father is with Me.—John 16:32 NKJV

God is love and to be God is to be very alone, for there is none like Him. This puts something lonely in love. It's a sacred trust. Love demanded solitudes of Christ. I demanded a loneliness of Him, even when multitudes were gathered about Him. A thing that none but He could understand. Love demanded of Him a cross fitted for one. Love demanded from Him a death, and death is lonelier still, for no one could accompany Him there. *As odd as it sounds, love is a strange loneliness that makes the heart full even with what it lacks. It is a thirst that is satisfied in its own thirstiness. Love is a lonely art. So is the surrender it must demand of each of us.*

In Christ, *warm life at the heart of solitude, Amen*

May you be the one constant in an inconstant world.

The Little Word
With the Big Heart

Say only yes if you mean yes, and no if you mean no.
  —*Matthew 5:37 NCV*

Yes. Yes. Yes. Yes. Yes. Choose any of them. Choose all of them.
It's yours. Do with it what you wish. Repeatable. Inexhaustible.
It gets stronger with use. It continually recreates, rebuilds,
compounds itself. Like a coin, spend it where it is necessary
and will do the most good for yourself or someone else.
Profit by it and feel no hesitation. Take it into your business,
to your home. Try it on your child, on your husband or wife.
Let it seek you out in the places where we secretly think of
ourselves. Keep it in your pocket for later use. Try it where
it may be least expected. Has God ever answered a prayer you
just knew was just too much to ask? Get the idea? Be the
instrument of joy and thankfulness to someone, all in the
industry of this little word with the big heart.

***Affirmatively in love, feverably, incorrigibly,
painstakingly in love, Amen***

Like the praisers and dancers that went before the army in
battle to summon up the Spirit of God, may your YES go
before you and may it rouse heaven on your behalf.

July 18

God looks down from heaven on the sons of men to see if there are any who understand, any who seek God.—Psalm 53:2 NIV

It's the most common of ailments. And the most hidden. It's not easily discerned, nor fixed, for it takes many shapes, wears many disguises. *Loneliness* should have no place in the House of Faith. Where lovers meet, there should be nothing to sustain it. The gathered warmth should be medicine enough. But why do my suspicions tell me otherwise? Why am I not convinced by what I see, what I know in my heart? *Lord, give me the wisdom to recognize and the strength to shake off what is artificial in me, the hollow, lifeless forms of love. Till my heart is free. Till the house I live in is a large, spacious, warm, and inviting house. Till Lonely is but a testimony among lovers. Till I love my neighbor as myself. Till my neighbor has the face love is known by, the voice love speaks with. I will not show up at Your door alone.*

In Jesus, the companion, Christ, and comfort of all the Eleanor Rigbys[11] hidden in my world, all the broken men, all the Father McKensies, Christ, the House I live in, Christ, the unlocked door, the light on in the hall, Christ, the key under the mat, the welcome written on my heart, Amen

A traveler's rest. Water to a pilgrim's thirst. May you say, "I would be a friend to your friends, O God."

11 *"Eleanor Rigby"—John Lennon & Paul McCartney*

THE REST OF MY LIFE

The LORD is my shepherd; I shall not want. He makes me to lie down in green pastures; He leads me beside the still waters. He restores my soul.—Psalms 23:1-3 NKJV

There is a rest in love. A pause, a trusting pause before a spinning world. A place of mending when the threads have come undone. *Lord, You calm my resisting soul. You hush the voice of urgency, of panic, of alarm. You call down severity, diminish need. You tender me to silence, loving, curing silence. Till the deep filaments of my body are still. Till the blood slows. O let me live in love's endless Sabbath. Let it follow me in all the tracks I make through this unsteady world. May I know when it calls to me. And let peace in me be generous, irresistible, catching in a world killing itself for the want of it.*

In Christ, the rest of my life, Amen

May silence be a welcomed event, a refuge, a regathering place. May it be a good defense. May you find God there and often.

LOVE AT FIRST SIGHT

JULY 20

"While I am in the world, I am the light of the world."
—*John 9:5 NCV*

Lord, by the strangest of rites You anointed the dead eyes of a man born blind and gave him sight. And his vision had intelligence, for he seemed in an instant to know You, not just the man who healed him, but the very God that gave vision to his life, that transformed him, that gave him the clarity and the bright joy that accompanies innocence reawakened. Love put a testimony in the mouth of blankness and silence. O love, be my vision. Transform the complete man in me. I am vacancy in need of substance. O, that my heart would glow with love's great heat, that this too dull and loveless world would brighten in its overflow. O, that I may be but spittle and dust in Your hands, Lord, before a world so desperately in need of sight.

In Christ, *love at first sight, **Amen***

May love overthrow all that has governed you till now, all the strong arguments by which your assessments are made, and with their expulsion, may you forget your former limits that accompanied them and allow love to establish new ones. May there be elastic in the seams.

DESPERATION: WHEN LOVE
FINDS ITS VOICE

For great is thy mercy toward me: and thou hast delivered my soul from the lowest hell.—Psalms 86:13 KJV

I'm not sure what hell will be like. Some say it is the absence of God. Others say flames and torment. I say I think I've been there and it was both. In the fervent heat, my illusions had little chance for survival, though they had been my previous hosts. There was nothing for them to feed upon any longer and they were perhaps the first things to go. I don't know. I wasn't paying attention to the order of things. But it was sufficient. I was lost and paralyzed in the deep seething mazes. But love, jealous for me, took up arms in my behalf, called down the dragon and slew it before my eyes. Out of the smoke and fury, I knew with certainty that *God is love* and I knew this great lyric in me was awakened at last, whose sweetness and whose echoes recoil upon me still.

> **In Him Who took up arms on my behalf,**
> **Christ, the love that overthrows me, Amen**

May you begin to know yourself purely, as love overthrows shame and other household myths.

CHRIST, TILL I BE FOUND AGAIN

For the Son of Man has come to save that which was lost.
  —Matthew 18:11 NKJV

Christ, when I am come undone.

Christ, when I have become but an unhappy distortion of myself.

Christ, when the stranger appears in my mirror, the phantom that shares my features, that speaks with my voice, that is filled out with my peculiar dimensions, but has no substance.

Christ, when I would burrow soul deep to lose myself for a time.

Christ, my needful Sabbath.

Christ, my requisite pause.

Christ, my shelter, this roof that bends above me.

Christ, these walls that compass me about.

Christ, the warm currents and eddies in my blood.

Christ, the temple within this temple.

Christ, if I am to lose myself,

And Christ, till I be found again.

May heaven grant you a Christ-sufficient life.

BUT THE JUST SHALL LOVE BY FAITH

Trust in the LORD with all your heart, and lean not on your own understanding; In all your ways acknowledge Him, and He shall direct your paths.—Proverbs 3:5-6 NKJV

Perhaps understanding love is irrelevant. Love is not among us to be understood. Love is here that we may live in God, that we may partake of Him in His essence, that we may live in echo of Him Who is Love. And the mystery is sufficient. It's the way He chose it to be, in spite of our attempts to deny Him of it, the mystery to which we would assign words, consigning to lists and catalogues the indescribable, unsearchable God. He won't be explained. The nature of divinity prohibits it. So it is with love. It won't be found in a house of words. It's too high for the senses that govern speech. It's too much God for us to utter this far below heaven. *But the just shall love by faith.*

In Christ, the faith it takes to love, and Christ, if understanding could come with but a word, Amen

May wonder and awe be your companion in growth, in rebirth, in the humblest of transformations, the most modest of changes. The simplest is beautiful, an outward witness to the inward God. It makes divinity conspicuous.

ROMANCE: FORGET SAFE!

JULY 24

Its flames are flames of fire, a most vehement flame. Many waters cannot quench love, nor can the floods drown it. If a man would give for love all the wealth of his house, it would be utterly despised.
—*Song of Solomon 8:6-7 NKJV*

Is fire safe? Is a hurricane favorable weather for planting rosebuds? When floods plunder your fields, is it time for a picnic? If you risk love, be advised of what you do. It's not safe. Forget safe. All of us have scars to prove this, scars that are chronicled, written on the heart as witness to the danger I now speak of, lessons we learned in our novitiate, in our youth when we believed all the songs, when our feelings overtook our brains, when we were captive to a wild and unmanageable heart and to the mystery of love, when we were willing slaves to this thing that felt so good and hurt so incredibly bad, the very day we began to build our fences, to spin and weave our counterfeit and our veils. *This is romance. It's a dangerous event. Ask Christ.*

In Christ, the wisdom necessary to love, Amen

May you never fear the risk of love. May you welcome it for the greater measure of faith required of you. Chance has no power over you. Love makes risk no risk at all. The giving of self is everything.

ROMANCE: THE TROUBLER

He brought me to the banquet room, and his banner over me is love.
  —Song of Solomon 2:4 NCV

There is a certain grace in the blood that makes romantic love romantic love, that makes it quite different from the love you would have for your grandmother, The Beatles, or a friend (though perhaps the same engine drives them all). This grace was designed by God at its most primal level, I suppose, to keep mankind going, replicating itself, peopling the earth. Romantic love is the most fragile, most volatile, most intimate, the most powerful of all expressions of love, and by His own words, it's what God desires with us. You can see it in the design of the temple. His inner chamber is sweet with perfumes, soft light, music, and fire. The stuff of love. So why call romance the troubler? Do I really need to answer that? What an odd thing, romantic love. How beautiful. Only God could have invented this.

In Christ, the oath I take, the life I give, Amen

May your day be a prayer in itself, a day that will not separate you from your Beloved.

JULY 26

I can do all things through Christ who strengthens me.
  —*Philippians 4:13 NKJV*

May a world that seemed impossibly big, that made you
feel so impossibly small, that loomed over you, that bullied
you about with indifference, whose valleys seemed too
dark, too long and too deep, whose mountaintops seemed
too unscalably high, may such a world shrink before you,
and give you advantage, that life may grow fat with possibility,
and the once untried, undared, unscaled, unthought, or
unattempted may become thinkable, workable, doable,
achievable.

In Christ, the thinkable, workable, doable, achievable, Amen

May Christ prove the impossible possible.

CHRIST, MY COMPLAINT

"Hear my prayer, O LORD, and give ear to my cry; Do not be silent at my tears; for I am a stranger with You, a sojourner, as all my fathers were."—Psalms 39:12 NKJV

I claim my rights to You, Lord, my rights of sanctuary, of citizenship, my rights of petition, of shelter, warmth, of hiding. You are my Sovereign, my chief city, the Jerusalem my soul seeks after. All roads in me, all inward paths lead to her hallowed gates. I am faint with suspense, for my soul is fixed on homeward gaze. I am sick with the sickness of the alien, the uncountried, as one far from his common and kindred earth. You are the complaint in me that is never still, the prayer that labors sweetly and unseen.

In Christ, my complaint, my unrest, Amen

May love be the rule established within you, the sovereignty to whom your fear is due. May God be seated in His rightful seat, Who we applaud by our acts, Who we worship in the daily routine of life.

WHO COULD HEAR ME?
I HAD SAID NOTHING.

JULY 28

…But the Spirit Himself makes intercession for us with groanings which cannot be uttered.—Romans 8:26 NKJV

I could not pray. I could not speak at all. I could not help but think of Him, though I could not rally words. My heart seemed broken against the rage of some invincible thing. Still, I know there is a place in me where love is enthroned, where love speaks freely and often to the God Who fathered it, in murmurs, in groans known only to love's secret ear. And in my silences, when the tongue wearies of itself, or when the elements have so spun me downward till I am collapsed in meek puddles of myself, I have access to Him Who loves me and my soul speaks with a clear and articulate voice to Him Who has purchased it for His own, Who hears me when I have no tongue to call upon Him. In love, He has given my soul rights to Him. In return, even as the heart of a maiden is hushed and sweet with submission, I have given Him rights to me.

In Christ, *when I could not speak for myself, Amen*

May the peace that accompanies prayer accompany you long after words are spent.

WHO COULD HEAR ME? I HAD
SAID NOTHING. A PRAYER

Now the Angel of the LORD found her[12] by a spring of water in the wilderness, by the spring on the way to Shur.—Genesis 16:7 NKJV

Who knows my soul's complaint before it can find shape upon my tongue? Who can perceive life stirring within me, like a thing unborn, that cannot speak for itself? You are the God Who hears me, Who misses no small thing. And though it is not unwelcomed, You do not need the sound of the human voice, the polish or the premeditation of words. Love alone hears what the heart cannot say, the things for which there is no language, all that is undeclared, unspoken. O my soul, uncoil your too long and silent spring. Merciful God, how foolish we are, how we trust the sound of our own voice. But I would rather be heard by You in the disturbed silence of my pain, than lose You in this waste of noise too common upon my lips.

In Christ, what heaven hears of me, Amen

May you discover the ceaseless spring. May you develop a thirst for her waters only.

---

12 *Hagar, who was pregnant with Ishmael, whose name means **God will hear**.*

LOVERS

I am my beloved's, and his desire is toward me.
  —Song of Solomon 7:10 NKJV

There is a mystical union, an agreement of essence that is no less than a marriage between you and God. And Christ is the event that makes this possible, that gives love rights to us, that fills our days with warmth and expectation, with wonder and bright promise, the dues of courtship. And though the word lover will rattle some of you, it's what we are becoming in Him, in our imitation of Him, in the very pattern of life that He has set before us, that we may warm the earth around us with this generous share of divinity. There is no other commission. Nor is there a greater one. Yeah, it rattles me. Daily.

**In Christ, the Church of the Incarnation,
where lovers meet, Amen**

May you seek communion with God even in the dullest of places, beneath the dimmest of lamps. And anywhere in this shrinking world, anywhere upon this swiftly spinning globe in the places where humanity gathers, may you have good brakes, may your engines slow to pause when life invites you inside.

When the Soul Needs a Sabbath

There remains therefore a rest for the people of God.
  —*Hebrews 4:9 NKJV*

May your soul be refreshed with an unexpected Sabbath,
a necessary pause, a rest, a replenishing of hidden stores.
May death and age be driven back another day, worry and
the overload of care be banished from your little kingdom.
May liberal Joy give you permission to play again, to dream,
to slow the times, to lengthen the day with blessedness. She
is beautiful. May she come to you with full hands.

In Christ, the Lord of the Sabbath, my day of rest and wonder, Amen

May you know true rest. May you recognize its voice when
it calls to you. May your body submit to the soft invitations
of quiet and stillness. And may you not fear to lose yourself
to the fascinations of a brook or the music of a human voice,
that charm the soul to its own calm ends. May you find a
Sabbath among the silk.

AUGUST

Christ, the knowable in God,
what I believe about love

WHAT I REALLY KNOW ABOUT WORSHIP I LEARNED FROM MY DOGS (PART ONE)

AUGUST 1

Thou shalt have no other gods before me.—Exodus 20:3 KJV

In the time I've known her, Savannah, my Dalmatian, has shown me more about worship, devotion, and selfless love than I have taken perhaps from a thousand sermons or as many worship songs. Dogs may be the only creature, man included, who love their masters more than they love themselves. She goes where I go, moves as I move, and without drawing attention to herself. You hardly notice she's even there. And being there is everything that matters to her. When I'm around, nothing else exists. It's like the first commandment is written in her blood. And I reward her with time, with slow ambling walks, and with long soft strokes of kindness. For her, worship is no less than the meaning of life itself, natural and deep, and takes so little thought of how to do it. It's just how she conducts her day. Selah. Paws.

In Christ, my selflessness, when love conducts the day before me, Amen

May you learn to love your Master more than yourself. May it take precedence in the blood. May your soul be His alone, yielded and obedient, warm and contented at His feet.

August 2

For every beast of the forest is Mine, and the cattle on a thousand hills. I know all the birds of the mountains, and the wild beasts of the field are Mine.—Psalms 50:10-11 NKJV

They can't judge me. Something in their blood won't let them. They can't refuse me either. Devotion denies them that art. My dogs love me in spite of what *I* know of me and in spite of the mystery I am to them. They fall all over themselves in a riot of pure joy if they see me coming or hear my voice. Their world is all right as long as it's peopled with me in it. *Presence is everything.* They count no wrongs against me. They have no plans to worry them. They have this indifference to wealth and gain that's hard to understand. And time is a *nonissue.* It's just not part of their sense of care. They enjoy a perpetual NOW. They can forgive with an ease you and I are incapable of (there's no grudge to hold if there's no time to keep it in). *O, if I could only love like that!*

In Christ, my Master, the one Voice I discern among the many, Amen

May Presence become everything to you. May the sound of His voice, His approaching footsteps, or the very sound of His name start a happy riot in your soul.

And Finally, It Was My Dogs Who Taught Me to Stop and Smell, well, everything!

Create in me a clean heart, O God; and renew a right spirit within me.
—*Psalms 51:10 KJV*

They never seem to labor or strive. They can sleep anywhere and on anybody's time—long lazy naps in the sun. Their conscience is purified of those things that complicate life. On long walks with any one of them, they have to stop at every flower, every bush, every growing and every lifeless thing and go through their routine inspections. I'm always impatient. They're just living life, full capacity in every moment. Loping along, doing what nature has put in them to do, and then living some more, doing it fully and in the confidence that devotion has bought for them. They're all gone now. Time and nature have taken them from me. I didn't know then that they were saying to me, *"STOP! And smell this, smell these roses, the plain, the withered, the beautiful, doesn't matter to me, this clump of dirt, ooh, what's this? mmmm! and this old shoe, this empty bottle, this puddle, this indistinguishable thing here… Isn't life good?!"*

In Christ, *anywhere love happens, any form it takes when it's real, Amen*

May life be *stick-your-head-out-of-the-car-window-let-the-wind-blow-in-your-face* kind of good!

AUGUST 4

An interpretation by way of litany from Psalms 68:1 KJV.

When all the elements of earth seem to conspire against you,
like wind and rain, or the thunder of too many tongues.

Let God arise, and let His enemies be scattered.

When the world seems to have changed and no one asked your consent.

Let God arise, and let His enemies be scattered.

When distraction or some unaccounted gloom
distances you from yourself.

Let God arise, and let His enemies be scattered.

When the Lilliputians of this world labor together to tie you
Gulliver-like down, when smallness tries to convince you of its strength
and the potency of its proud cables,

Let God arise, and let His enemies be scattered.

The day is yours by a promise more lasting than all myths and fables,
all charges and accusations this world can summon against you,

Let God arise, and let His enemies be scattered.

So, by the love that gently mocks at time,
that carries us endlessly through it,

Let God arise, and let His enemies be scattered.

May God arise. And may that be sufficient.

LOVE AND VISUAL EFFECTS

One thing I know: that though I was blind, now I see.
—*John 9:25 NKJV*

With my wife, there are times I think I see the child.
A delicate, unexplored, and private passage opens to me
alone, and in wonder I see the innocence that hides itself,
laughing, playing, frightened, lost. She allows me. She's not
afraid for love to divine her secrets. *Transparency is the rule
of exchange and gives love rights to us. It allows love to be itself
between us, to search our souls with the eye of timeless divinity.*
She allows me to haunther shadows, to gently prowl among
what ruins there may be, to chase away her demons, real
or imagined, with nothing more at times than an embrace
or a wordless kiss, soft as a prayer, a touch that makes reply
to some deep and unanswered question in her. We have no
need of veils, for this refound paradise, this nakedness, this
divine and necessary light has found sanctuary between us.

In Christ, this paradise where love can be itself, Amen

May you see beyond given shapes and forms, beyond what
you know. May your vision be greater than the habits of your
mind, higher than your fences, stronger than the voices that
spend themselves in the debating places of the heart.

WORSHIP AND THE CLOUD
OF MY UNDOING

AUGUST 6

*...The priests could not continue ministering because of the cloud;
for the glory of the LORD filled the house of the LORD.*
— 1 Kings 8:11 NKJV

Worship is the fulfillment of our deeper humanity. It gathers
us heavenward, crowds us upward, outside ourselves and
into a holy place. *The youthful John quiet upon the breast of
His Master.* Incited by God, it draws the soul to its source
of origin, where the cloud is thick and reason is overthrown.
It arises from that place within us where longing abides,
where psalms are bred, where ecstasy broods like untended
fire. *O, let worship flourish, let it prosper in me, unending, filtering
into the very lengths and limits of me, into the full sum of who
I am, body and soul, brain and marrow. May I know less and less
where You begin, Lord, and where I end, that You-ness and I-ness
fade into blissful one-ness.*

**In Jesus, the Lamb, the sacrifice of myself, this martyrdom
turned to music, worship within me mounting up, all that is yet
undeclared, all that is unvoiced still, Christ, to Whom all the
reverence and all the substance of this one life is due, Amen**

May your mind quiet in the act of worship. May the cloud
be too thick for words, too rich for thought.

The Warm Center of His Mystery

To all perfection I see a limit; but your commands are boundless.
—Psalms 119:96 NIV

May you realize—by an awareness you trust and know to be faithful, even when your suspicions say otherwise, when logic and order have better arguments, or in a time when you have come to the weary borders of yourself, where the connecting threads are thin and worn with use, where hope is brittle, and the heart is sick with delay, nevertheless, and by a sense you can't quite place, by a name you can't quite say, by an eternity you can't quite understand—may you be assured, by a deep and immovable conviction, that *God has not changed His mind about you,* that indeed, His mind is set on you, by an unbreakable bond, an unbendable law, that He is as much the pilgrim and you the pilgrimage of His heart, and that you alone are the warm center of His mystery, the desire that weighs sweet against His breast.

In Christ, what God thinks of me, Amen

May a generous heaven confound your lack of faith with wonder and substance.

You Don't Resume Life Here.
You Remember It.

AUGUST 8

I remember the days of old…—Psalms 143:5 NKJV

It was used as an army hospital during the Civil War and is now
a retreat center operated by the Episcopal Church. It's large and
airy, spacious, with high ceilings and old wood. An old world,
with newer paint. Creaking staircases still resonant with secrets
and the hum of forgotten life, with rails smooth with use, with
history, and the traffic of hands. Ghosts and the spell of old Time
prowl all around you. The smell of antiquity, of oldness, distant,
faint, and yet inescapable, a smell you can't quite place, one that
plays with the memory. There was no phone, no TV, no internet
and no noise (other than nature itself), no air conditioning in
the rooms (although cool nights and pleasant mountain days
diminished any complaint and called back something genuine to
the senses). No locks on the doors. No Starbucks®. Cell phones
wouldn't work. I brought habit and custom with me and I
wrestled a bit when I had to lay them down. But it was Okay.
You don't really resume your life in such a place. You remember it.

In Christ, *my reconciliation, the sweet come again, Amen*

When love demands surrender, may you leave no traces of
your former self, no root nor stem by which such a life may
spring again.

When I am Overwhelmed—A Prayer

...When my heart is overwhelmed; lead me to the rock that is higher than I.—Psalms 61:2 NKJV

Grant me peace when I am overwhelmed, Lord, when the noise and traffic of this day prove too much for me. May love be a shelter, a refuge, a quiet room where I may secret myself away even in the heat of this day's activity. When I am a target, an easy mark for distraction, be my shield, my hidden armor. Love, be wisdom in me today, my angel, my rear guard, the sweet counsel I take, the well I draw water from. And at the end of this day, when the skies are weary of the sun, when my body is weary with labor, may love be the open door into night as it wakens the soft light of our houses, as it sweetens our conversation and the normal business of living, the ceramic clink of our plates being put away, the emptying of our last warm cups, the dying music and the slow decline of evening. May love pilot me into my own spaces, into my fellowship of dreams and slumbers sweet with mystery and the opiates that quiet me in the dark and sleepward night.

In Christ, my quiet room, my unending day, Amen

May heaven put to flight the troubler of your peace, any unwelcomed guest within your little house. You are more beautiful to God than all creation that preceded you, more precious to heaven than the angels that people it.

CLUELESS

I will instruct you and teach you in the way you should go; I will guide you with My eye.—Psalms 32:8 NKJV

Surrendering to love is to accept life at its highest expression, life as it was designed to be. In a doubting day, an untrusting day, in a day when faith and certitude seems anemic and pale, we may trust in love, for love alone cannot fail, no matter how the day may be reflected once we have looked back upon it.

So clueless let me ever be, for love is watching over me,

To love alone I risk my soul, surrender absolute control,

If you would dare to know love's mind, not to fear what you may find

If you suspect that love is true, then love may find a home in you,

And all who look upon these lines,

Who endure these poor distracted rhymes,

Who choose to Love with no regret, may prove to be a lover yet.

In Christ, *love's best version of itself,* **Amen**

May love be deeper than instinct, finer than thought.

I would have lost heart, unless I had believed that I would see the goodness of the LORD in the land of the living. Wait on the LORD; be of good courage, and He shall strengthen your heart; wait, I say, on the LORD!—Psalms 27:13-14 NKJV

Shepherd me, O God. Let love pilot me in my soul's search for itself. Till I find my true mirror. Till the day of Christ in me. Free me of my myths, all my illusions. Free me of the Judas who would starve my world of its warmth for coin, whose kisses are cold, whose dark betrayals would leave my soul in shadows of itself, seeking mirrors that tell nothing.

In Christ, the answer in the glass, Amen

May there be little question as to this phenomenon of you. May it be clear and wonderful in your eyes, even as it is in the eye of heaven. May there be no debate within the heart when you consider who you are, when you consider what heaven and earth have so beautifully and so meticulously crafted together by design and by bold innovation.

I am Holy (Part One)

August 12

And because of this, we are made holy through the sacrifice Christ made in his body once and for all time.—Hebrews 10:10 NCV

A good confession: *I am Holy to the Lord. Consecrated. Washed. Robed. Made perfect in His sacrifice. I did not choose Him. He chose me. When He looks upon me, something moves deep in His heart. He has set me at His banqueting table and His banner over me is love. I am the Lord's and He is mine. He withholds no good thing from me. He sees Himself reflected in me and love is not blind. And if I sustain any other vision, if I see myself any other way, I reduce His gift, I hold it in contempt. But I am bound to Him with a deathless and unbreakable bond. Therefore, I will speak with the tongue of the redeemed. I will conduct my life as one bought back from death, for Christ closed the distance between God and me.*

**In Christ, my holiness, this vow I live,
this vision I keep, Amen**

May you be able to look inward and not shrink, knowing that it is no less a holy place, the habitation of God.

I am Holy (Part Two)

And you shall be holy to Me, for I the LORD am holy, and have separated you from the peoples, that you should be Mine.
—Leviticus 20:26 NKJV

Lord, I am like a man who has lived in darkness, who sees light for the first time and cannot endure it. I am sick with love, and do not know what is happening to me. I am a child in my understanding. I am a child in love. Come to me sweetly, O Christ. Your words are medicine to my soul. You have said in Your heart, "This one is Mine." You have said to me, "You are Holy." You have silenced my best arguments, broken my shields, pierced my reflective armors. Your love has so beaten down my wall of defense against You, and in the rubble, I think I see traces of Your blood. Enter my gates now as one who conquers a city, for I am a defenseless people. Thank You for the love that overpowers me, that sees no barrier, that respects no wall, that holds my life more precious than its own.

In Christ, my life in overwhelm, Amen

May holiness put life back in harness. May it shepherd you to rightness again.

AUGUST 14

I call to remembrance my song in the night; I meditate within my heart, and my spirit makes diligent search.—Psalms 77:6 NKJV

During a heavy storm not long ago, my son asked, "Why do these things seem to happen more at night?" I said, *"It gives writers something to do."* Truth is, a dark night, a hard rain, and an unquiet heart is enough to make me lyrical. I suspect your devotional practice varies from day to day like my own, a thing as fluid as life. A prayer. A worthy read. A random act of kindness. A quiet moment with a journal— life tunneling itself outward in meticulous and inky little stabs. Or praise that sweetens the hour with music and lightness. And sometimes there is nothing, a nothing so rich you struggle against it, an emptiness that has life and sense. Then sometimes there is just nothing, stark nothing. *So let life be life! And let love be the sun that warms your day, the night that teaches you how to dream!*

In Christ, *life as it was meant to be, love as it should be,* **Amen**

May love put words in your mouth, warmth in your eyes, and a prayer to roam the vast and sacred tenements of the heart, till it be filled, till it speaks.

DOUBT: A SHEPHERD'S STAFF, A CLOUD TO TELL ME WHERE THE RAIN IS

AUGUST 15

For we walk by faith, not by sight.—2 Corinthians 5:7 NKJV

If only we could unravel the mystery of heavenly things
by reason. If only love was reasonable. If only we could
understand God the way a mathematician understands
numbers and formulas, or that we could rally our deeper
senses the way a lawyer makes an argument, or in the curious
way a scientist looks into a microscope. *But we can't.* If only
love could be assessed and attained by an exercise of mind.
If only God could be known by mental ascent and that
all possibilities of doubt could be harnessed and eliminated.
But they can't. We are not being fashioned as lawyers,
mathematicians, or even theologians. We are being made into
lovers. And for lovers, doubt is not the enemy we suspect it
is. It puts caution in my steps, reverence into the pulse of life.
It tells me with some assurance that I am not God, especially
in an age trying so desperately to convince itself otherwise.
Doubt: it's a shepherd's staff. It's a cloud to tell me where the rain is.

In Christ, love beyond a reasonable doubt, Amen

May your faith be a gift to be unwrapped, not a secret to
figure out.

YES: WHAT'S IN A NAME?

AUGUST 16

The yes to all of God's promises is in Christ, and through Christ we say yes to the glory of God.—2 Corinthians 1:20 NCV

Perhaps the Germans came closest to getting it right. Their word for YES is 'ja,' even as it sounds to us in the name *Yah-weh*. And what about the Hebrew *'Jeshua'* (pronounced with a Yes as in *Yeshua*), the Latinate *'Iehovah,'* the Greek *'Iesous,'* pronounced YEAH'-soos or YAY'-soos? Okay, it's close enough! These are the first of all first syllables, the first in a name by which we name the unnamable God, what the tongues of our ancestors could only shape in their mouths as the primal YES. *And O, the joy of praying to the God Whose answer was in His name, Who is the One and Omnipositive, the All and Absolutely, the Divine and Affirming YES-I-AM, the Mighty and Irrevocable YES-I-WILL, the YES-YOU-CAN and the O-YES-YOU-ARE!*

In Christ, the One and Omnipositive, YES and Amen

May the Jesus in you resonate with YES, for yourself as well as others who would ask it of you. May He be the AMEN, the 'SO BE IT' of all your requests.

LOVE WITHOUT THINKING

He was oppressed and He was afflicted, yet He opened not His mouth; He was led as a lamb to the slaughter, and as a sheep before its shearers is silent, so He opened not His mouth.—Isaiah 53:7 NKJV

Some time ago, I asked my oldest son to tell me about God but without the use of words. Taken a bit off guard, he just stared back at me through dimples and grins. His wife, sitting nearby, caught on, I think, and said to him, "Give him a hug!" A portrait in warmth. It was primal. And sufficient. My son's first instinct was to think. Most of us keep our faith in the same place language dwells, where we catalog things, record things, give titles and names to things, where we separate things one from another, and figure things out, where we keep our arguments, and where we trade the most. But love isn't so easily confined to such a place. Love is outside mind. Outside reason. It's heart. All heart. God is love. Demonstrate Him. In a language outside of language. Touch without seeing. Love without thinking.

In Christ, love's deepest instinct, that makes language unneccesary, Amen

May you be like the soundless harp, where music waits, the stillness in the strings He alone may search with His interrogating fingers.

AUGUST 18

My son, give attention to my words; incline your ear to my sayings. Do not let them depart from your eyes; Keep them in the midst of your heart; for they are life to those who find them, and health to all their flesh. Keep your heart with all diligence, for out of it spring the issues of life.—Proverbs 4:20-23 NKJV

We weave the fictions of our lives with words. We create our household myths with them. We are responsible or we are reckless with them in our traffic and trade. They are coin in the market place where the soul disperses itself. They can enlarge or diminish life. They have the power to inspire, to promote life and wonder. Words are medicine. Or they are sickness in my bones. *Did I build a cathedral, a holy place from my words, or did I let ill report build a hovel or a house of straw? Words. Only love can turn them into music. And by a process we still don't understand.*

In Christ, *the language I choose to disperse myself, Amen*

May God make light of your words, enough to illumine a dim world.

LOVE AND FAITH

If we are faithless, He remains faithful; He cannot deny Himself!
  —2 Timothy 2:13 NKJV

Love doesn't need me to believe in order to exist or to
operate in my life any more than God does. Like truth, love is
not subject to what I believe. It remains love. It has no choice.
Its divinity is too strong, too fixed. And no more than I can
understand the mystery of God, can I understand the mystery
of love. That makes faith necessary in love. It provides what
understanding cannot. Love gives faith something to do. It
puts faith to its best use, its highest vocation. *To be a man of
God is to be a man in love, and that is a man of faith.*

**In Christ, the knowable in God, what I believe about love,
Amen**

May your faith be gregarious, extroverted, and engaging.
May your beliefs be believable. May your faith be waterproof,
tamperproof, bugproof, foolproof, fireproof, idiotproof,
condition, and compromiseproof. May it be teflon coated,
scotchguarded. And may your faith be the kind you'd take
home to your mother. May it be magnetic, that would stick
with pride upon any refrigerator door.

SUDDENLY AND AGAIN

AUGUST 20

Though an army may encamp against me, my heart shall not fear;
though war should rise against me, in this I will be confident.
  —*Psalms 27:3 NKJV*

I woke up early with the expectation of plenty. Perhaps
I should have slept in. Expectation of a thing is not the
thing itself. The way before me became suddenly and again a
mystery. And yet I will not be alarmed, for I am no stranger
to faith, nor to its twin escort, hope, who as it guides, will
lead me through the maze, through all the unsprung traps,
and through all the anxious flusters of the day. *Love will keep*
its appointments, those known and unknown to me, and I will look
back, as I have a thousand times in wonder, and see that all was
in its place, that time was not too early nor too late, that love was
master of every detail, and that between love and me, at least one
of us was behaving as they should.

In Christ, the Master of accounts, Amen

May fear find no consent at all, no permissions in you, not
the slightest loophole.

Rabboni

But without faith it is impossible to please Him, for he who comes to God must believe that He is, and that He is a rewarder of those who diligently seek Him.—Hebrews 11:6 NKJV

We're all going to have days when love seems impossible, days when it seems that the closer we come to love, to life-sustaining warmth, the more aloof it becomes, distancing itself from us altogether, necessitating a faith that just doesn't seem to be there, a faith that seems to have gone south, leaving me chill and comfortless. But there is a hidden spring. There is a sure deposit, a sharing of essence, a *Christ life* in each of us that is separate, distinct from us, and yet, fully our own, nested deep and immovable in the heart's core. Love can be my host and my instruction through those dull, vexing, and seemingly loveless days. I am the student. I am youth in love.

In Christ, Rabboni, when love seems impossible, Amen

May you welcome Christ in all the winding currents of your day. May He labor with you, ever a servant, ever God.

Till Him:
An Ecstasy of the Hopeful

August 22

…That you may approve the things that are excellent, that you may be sincere and without offense till the day of Christ…
—Philippians 1:10 NKJV

Till love be love in us at last. Till His name only. Till all argument is purged in love's jealous heat. Till all our paths conjoin to one singular and observable way. Till love alone be the detectable difference we make in this indifferent world. Till we are a people set apart, marked by love and lowliness, humility and gentleness, by warmth and by kindness, kindness that has no thought of itself, love with no thought of reward but love itself. Till Him.

In Christ, my full heart, Amen

May the world see and understand that the house of God is a big rambling warm cozy house. May they recognize it by the name it goes by, that is, your own.

THE PRICE OF PASSAGE

*I am a stranger in the earth; do not hide Your commandments from
me. My soul breaks with longing for Your judgments at all times.*
  —*Psalms 119:19-20 NKJV*

*Lord, when I read the prayers of your servants, an echo sounds
deep within me. I too am a stranger here. I am uncountried. I follow
another rule. I live by an inward law that I cannot fully understand
and yet I know the way is marked with blood and tenderness.
Such love is too wonderful for me, and yet, is in every way my
own. Christ is the debt I owe in this world. Christ is the price of
citizenship for the next. Love will shepherd me there, to that far
country to which my allegiance and all my oaths tend even now.
My heavy toll is paid, my fare bloodbought. Love is my debt even as
it is my reward. Love, I am your countryman. Be my fellow sojourner
and let us speak in the tongue of our Fatherland. And Lord, grant me
a quiet heart where I may retreat in peace in the unquiet hour.*

In Christ, the price of passage, Amen

May you come to know the peace which faith purchases in
quietness and in yielding.

LOVE AND MIND

AUGUST 24

But we have the mind of Christ.—*1 Corinthians 2:16 NKJV*

There is nothing like the mind of man. Nor is there anything
quite so difficult to harness. It contains multitudes. It contains
worlds, nations born and unborn, and kingdoms, some yet
to be imagined, inventions for a world we have yet to know,
and the literature that will inspire and redeem some distant
moment of idling time. The mind of man is godlike in this
capacity, an echo of the deity that thought it up. All minds are
capable. Whatever limits or restraints there may be, are usually
self-imposed. The mind of man was designed in love and
designed for love, to operate within the rule and government
of love, and it is capable of understanding timelessness, infinity,
intimacy, selflessness, obedience, holiness—all the things that
are restored to us in the mind of Christ.

**In Christ, *heaven's most treasured thought invested in me,
Amen***

May love cleanse your mind of its misbelief, of its fictions,
of any untruths, replenish it with joy, with beauty, with
nobility, and secrets from the treasure house that the mind
cannot yet understand.

Oh, send out Your light and Your truth! Let them lead me; let them bring me to Your holy hill and to Your tabernacle.
—Psalms 43:3 NKJV

To be honest is a fearful thing. To be innocent in a world that has long lost its innocence seems too much to ask. It's just not civilized. We are asking a prying world to judge, to investigate, to question, to make commentary upon every blemish, every ugly and unclean thing about us. To be true, to be without cunning, to be without concealments, is to impose banishment upon ourselves in a world of imitation, forgery, and imposture. It is so tempting, rather, to let some invention, some imagined likeness of ourselves speak for us, and tell a curious world, *"This is who I am."* And yet, in that same moment, our oaths deflate, our devotion becomes but an exercise, our worship only music, and love, a lonely imitation.

In Christ, our uncivilized God, Amen

May you give others the rare liberty to be themselves. It's a gift so few expect, that gives the world back its originality, a Christianity without veils, humanity free to discover its authentic self.

ONE WAY

He has shown you, O man, what is good; and what does the LORD require of you but to do justly, to love mercy, and to walk humbly with your God?—Micah 6:8 NKJV

Love has only one way. And, as it can be said of all things that have their source, their genesis in God, it is good. And though it is good, it is not good by our assessment of what is good, for love is good according to its own measure of goodness, by the laws it has set against itself, unbreakable and true, a goodness that is as solid and as fixed as heaven itself, as the very throne of God, upon which we may put our whole trust. God is good. In all things, we can say God is good. And He's not obligated to us for consent. He doesn't need our permission nor our counsel to be Himself. Perhaps a certain indifference, a certain dispassion, is what He seeks from us, that we can be found content in whatever situation we are in, that we may say 'it is good.'

In Christ, *the Lord of my contentment,* **Amen**

May this very day show its goodness to you. May suspense and joy, ecstasy and anticipation command the currents and all swiftly running streams that warm the heart.

In Want and Wandering

...He has scattered the proud in the imagination of their hearts.
—*Luke 1:51 KJV*

Lord, we have imagined love as we wanted love to be. In our loneliness, we sought its face, its voice. We sought its shelters, its concealments to cover our nakedness. We were strangers upon the earth and to the God that made it. Love cried out to us in the wilderness, still, we were afraid, even as men who fear the unknown, as one may fear the light who lives in darkness, as one who fears to wake when the dream seems sweet and true. Redeem my soul from its want, from its care, from its slumbers, from seeking for itself alone. Rouse me, Lord, that I may no longer sleep, that I may no longer be captive to the dream, to the sweet sorcery of pretended love. Let love awaken in me. Summon my life back from the dead, from the nothingness, from the dull oblivions of sleep. May the understanding of my heart be refashioned, recreated, reborn in love.

In Christ, love that never sleeps, Amen

May love be a watcher on your walls and parapets, a sentinel where you dream.

LOVE EASY IN ME

AUGUST 28

Whoever says that he lives in God must live as Jesus lived.
  —*1 John 2:6 NCV*

If God told me to imitate Him, the capacity for such a command must exist within me as more than mere possibility. More than the stuff of habit, I suspect love is closer to nature itself within us. A nature too deep, a divinity too denied, it may just be burrowed, nested somewhere within or just outside my understanding, hidden, filed away, a part of my truer identity that I lost in the noise and distractions of this present age. Perhaps it's a matter of waking. *Or remembering.* That love may be the involuntary, the inevitable, the autonomic response to life, authentic nature expressing itself, *love easy in me.*

In Christ, my remembered nature, Amen

May your words be little builders, having within them the soul of the architect and not the wrecking crew.

THAT I MAY KNOW HIM

That I may know him, and the power of his resurrection, and the
fellowship of his sufferings, being made conformable unto his death.
  —Philippians 3:10 KJV

Lord, give me wisdom and a mouth to put it in, a hopeful
congregation of words and ink to wash it from me. I want to know
Christ, in the loving, where He is to be found. I want to know Him
in the surrender not yet complete in me. I want to behold Him alone
when love awakens my heart and opens my sleeping eyes. O that
I may know love beyond the dull and lifeless forms of our religion
and the ornaments we dress it with. That I may know the person,
the essence, the source and spring, the very Him my soul longs for
and before Whom I utter this complaint.

In Christ, *this pressing ache of love within my breast,* **Amen**

And when understanding comes, in its time, may you be
as one who wakes, as one who delights in the sudden
understanding of a proverb or in the loosened knot of a
riddle. May you be as one who takes joy in the unraveling
of a poem, when the mystery, the one and lovely parable
of your one and lovely life, begins to unfold.

LOVE AND WINNING

AUGUST 30

Love never fails.—1 Corinthians 13:8 NKJV

The truest success is found in that alone which cannot fail.
I suspect only love can make such an outrageous claim and
mean it. But love is evolved humanity, man elevated, advanced
government, true Christianity, no less than a vision of life.
Winning and losing, success and failure decline into irrelevance
in the lover's soul. There is only love. Human glory is absorbed
in the greater light of love. And love is always successful, in
spite of appearances, in spite of the usual measures by which
we measure success in our world. In a show of largeness, love
may ask you to lose in a contest where you know you can
win, where glory is but a chalk line away. Love may ask you
to be second when you know you could be first. You may be
asked to surrender your one life even in the knowledge that
the God Who created this big world is at the very center of
that life. And for love alone. Sounds Jesus to me.

**In Christ, my trophy, my shining treasure, the torch aflame
and burning in my hands, Amen**

Excellence, yes. Distinction, yes. But may you come to know,
even as the martyrs before you knew, what it truly means to win.

HEART, MIND, AND CHRIST
IN THE MIDST OF THEM

For where two or three are gathered together in my name, there am I in the midst of them.—Matthew 18:20 KJV

When heart and mind struggle against each other, as they will in this intolerant, odd and misbelieving world, when they contend with one another as for dominance, may the heart prove itself unequalled in challenges, and yet, may it prove itself a benevolent conqueror, the seat of a kind and holy God, giving light and alliance to the mind, offering its good counsel in a time of decision, *remembering that only in love are the two united again according to the original design of Him Who created you.*

In Jesus, the Christ in the midst of them, Amen

May you know the joy of Eden again, the lost earth of our nativity where the heart and mind kept better company, where they lived together in perfect concord, where nature itself was church enough for man, where harmony held all things together, where love and creation were inseparable, and where innocence thought so little of any of these things.

SEPTEMBER

Christ, love that came to us like music,
that burned in us like fire

LOVE AND THE RESPONSIBLE LIFE

Love must be sincere.—*Romans 12:9 NIV*

*Lord, help me to be responsible in love today, to be love's good
steward, love's wise ambassador, love's faithful servant. When I feel
nothing, let love prove itself larger than feelings, larger than influence
or habit, larger than any power that would rule over me, inward or
outward. Give me the wisdom to be simple, to take the complications
out of my relationships, the mystery out of my actions, the riddle
from my speech, so love can have an easy voice in me. And give me
advancement in Your kingdom, this heaven on earth where love is
Imperial, where it enjoys undoubted rule, where salvation dwells and
gives generously of itself, where Wisdom chooses to reside and keep
her counsel.*

In Christ, how I am to behave, Amen

May love bring out the better stuff in you, showing humanity
where it is evolving. May you be Christ to those who have
none, no less than Jesus to those in need of warmth.

TABLE TALK: LOVE AND RELIGION
(PART ONE)

SEPTEMBER 2

You prepare a table before me in the presence of my enemies…
  —Psalms 23:5 NKJV

It's just you and your cappuccino, musing together, divining dreams in the foam. Then Religion finds you. He comes with all the appearance of friendship and with the high noble front of spirituality. So, with a smile you offer him a place at your table. He's affable enough, sharp, quick, but a little too ready for a contest of words or ideology. *He's right and he knows he's right.* He comes to sell, to put his order first. He is surrendered only to that. You are second, a prize, an enlistment, a trophy to be won. His agenda, which is inflexible and intolerant, will not hide for long and eventually the inevitable happens, as it must when Religion sits at your table—*lines emerge.* Dividing ones. Argument raises its voice. You are either ally or enemy. Nothing more. Religion proves himself but a tiresome guest. He's an argument and I think he's rather silly. A whirlwind has just passed and you notice your cup has cooled in your hands.

> **In Christ, Who champions me, silence
> in the throat of argument, Amen**

May argument have no asylum in you, no jurisdiction, no pulpit, no consents, and no place to feed.

SEPTEMBER 3

You anoint my head with oil; My cup runs over.—Psalms 23:5 NKJV

Love, on the other hand, comes to your table. Soft. Selfless.
Inquisitive without imposition. In suggestion, not overthrow.
With invitations, not demand. *It comes to you with all the rights
of divinity and yet with all the humility and authenticity of a warm
human Christ seeking to give of itself in absolute benefit of you.*
No lines. No arguments. It's too surrendered for that, too
elevated, too evolved, too truly Christian, too much taken
by the mystery of you and with a overt longing to celebrate
that mystery, to realize it with you and to have you celebrate
it yourself. And there is no sequence, no procession, no first
or second in love. There is only you. Love spans multitudes,
times, and worlds. Still, there is only you. That's love's own
mystery. *O love, be the good medicine of my better health. Keep
stern and stifling Religion far from me, banish it from my house,
with all its arguments.*

In Christ, the warmth returned to my cup, Amen

May you never fear moments of tenderness, in giving or
in receiving, nor the authority by which they come in
an untender world.

THE GOD OF ASSENT AND ASCENT

SEPTEMBER 4

*"You have seen what I did to the Egyptians, and how I bore
you on eagles' wings and brought you to Myself."*
  —Exodus 19:4 NKJV

Assent: a YES, an agreement. Ascent: a rising, an elevating.
In love, one is not possible without the other. They are,
in fact, inseparable, not unlike the cherubim whose wings
overspread the Ark, where the terms of agreement, the assent
of Heaven is kept. *Loose these weights from me, Lord, all my
hoarded things, this guarded life, this heaviness of mortality, this
excess gravity of the heart, all my unnecessary bindings. Love,
be lightness in me, youth again, weightless and winged. Let my
soul ascend. Let it rise heavenward for the brief remainder of my
days, like perfume in dispersion, like prayer set aloft in the ear of
paradise. Be my upwardness, Lord, my heart's ambition. O, for the
beating of wings, for an angel to pry the lock that seals the thick
closure of my heart, all at the delicious sound of YES as it rises.*

In Christ, my soul by assent ascending, Amen

I bid you Christ! And may He loose the heart of its
bindings, of all its bars and confinements, all that has kept
you in and kept others out.

SUNDAY, MONDAY, AND ALWAYS

Satisfy us in the morning with your unfailing love, that we may sing for joy and be glad all our days.—Psalms 90:14 NIV

Where is the Sunday that came and went? Where is the drowsy napping afternoon, with all its sorceries of music and the redeeming lull of conversation with those we love, those to whom we gathered ourselves in the sweet passing of the one and unguarded day? *Lord, Sundays are sweet with the grace of rest, with an allowable ease. There is agreement in nature it seems, a medicine that disperses itself in the elements. O for that time when time meant nothing, when we seemed not to notice, when we played, when we acted on our immediate and deeper impulses, when we considered not the risks of life, when angels and steeples were more interesting because of our crayon Sunday mornings. When we laughed ourselves stupid and cried ourselves empty. When we were unreasonable. When we were free. When we were young. When we needed a good Father above us.*

**In Jesus, my endless Sunday, and
Christ of Mondays too, Amen**

May you forgive your own youth in its struggle for life.

WHAT CAN BE SAID FOR TUESDAY?

SEPTEMBER 6

This is the day the LORD has made; we will rejoice and be glad in it.—Psalms 118:24 NKJV

What can be said for Tuesday? What music is there in the word itself? It's a whole day removed from the wide, breath-fetching yawn of the day before, from Monday's sleepy optimism, the catatonic *where-am-I?-limb-stretching-first-day-back-in-harness*. And it's not the *summit-topping-flag-planting-I've-made-it-this- far* middle of the week. Nor is it the happier *week-in-decline-it's-almost-over-I-feel-Friday-rockin'-in-my-blood*. It's just Tuesday. Churches feast on Wednesdays. Thursday is a descent, a pleasant downward slope, a tunnel with evidence of light at the end of it. But Tuesday? It's just not that interesting of a day. Not a bad day. Just Tuesday. But there's poetry in the plainest of days, greatness disguised in ordinary clothes. Tuesday may just have a voice worth waiting for that's all her own. Love doesn't care for calendars and the day ain't over yet.

In Jesus, the God of Tuesdays as well, Amen

May love add spontaneity, suspense, and anticipation to the general stream of life, so much that even the dull and commonplace begin to take on something sacred about them.

WHAT CAN BE SAID FOR TUESDAY?
A PRAYER

*Every day I will bless You, and I will praise Your name forever
and ever.—Psalms 145:2 NKJV*

*Lord, what a silly tribute I have made to the unfortunate name
of Tuesday. Outcast. An exile in the lists of merrier days. Prove me
wrong, O Majesty, Sovereign of all days, Timeless God! Put music
in the bashful mouth of Tuesday. Where we would not expect it,
where we would not have stopped to listen, let the day sing even
as one sings when the heart is light. Come, Lord, undo this sad
tribute. It reveals me. I am found out in my words. Father, quiet
the complaints that steal something beautiful from any of my days.
Redeem the time, O Lord. Let love be about its usual labors, its
usual transformations in me. Sweeten the name of Tuesday in the
record of my heart, for it will return again, and will no doubt ask
something of me. Let such a day find its song in me at last. I am
but lines, notes, and stops, eager for sound.*

**In Christ, the silencer of my complaints,
the poetry of Tuesdays, Amen**

May blessedness in you shape itself to words, to an audible
kiss. And may it possess divinity enough to make princes of
frogs or to wake beauty where she sleeps.

PRAYER: AN INNERVIEW

SEPTEMBER 8

My God will hear me.—Micah 7:7 NKJV

Prayer, a single grain of sand, grit within my shell that promises a pearl. It is a laborer within my secret world, who must toil among my memories, rummage among my forgotten things, traffic among my ghosts, among the detritus and wreckage of dreams, who must frequent the place where anger keeps its accounts and where the prisoners of my unforgiveness lay, those with no one to speak for them, to loose them from the unkindness of their bonds. Prayer is an agent, a broker in this private innerview between God and me, an appointed ambassador who does His bidding, makes the odd rounds, undoes the hidden knot and confesses me at last.

**In Christ, the Jesus it takes for my soul
to voice its way to God, Amen**

May inwardness show you the wonder of things, the wonder of who you are. May it be a familiar retreat in a time of necessity. May God occupy all your rooms.

INK ENOUGH

Heaven and earth will pass away, but My words will by no means pass away.—Matthew 24:35, Mark 13:31, Luke 21:33 NKJV

You moved princes and peoples. You unsettled mountains and monarchs. All with a word. You cursed the branches of the hoarding tree. You called the elements to account when Your sleep was disturbed, made an unquiet sea quiet again. You rebuked the rage in the pent-up skies and took away its conviction, its howl. You are the Author of life itself Whose words are fit with fire and lightning, with wonder and tenderness, with groaning thunder and command. Yours was the necessary signature that would seal the treaty between heaven and earth and end the enmity between them. Your blood was ink enough. I am warm for words.

In Christ, love that bled with rule and wonder, Amen

May you be comforted in the knowledge that His first effort, the great evidence of His handiwork still shines as bright around you, His earth lay just as steady under you, that galaxies and hidden suns are set firm in their courses above you, that His air still busies your lungs with breath, that His waters still quiet your thirst, His bread stills your hunger, that His corrections still shepherd you, His encouragements and His rewards quicken your soul with delight.

WHEN WORDS WON'T COME

For the sake of my brethren and companions, I will now say,
"Peace be within you."—Psalms 122:8 NKJV

If you choose a life that is inward and upward, a life
of the spirit, silence will be one of the first articles in your
catechism. Silence, like no other state or event, provokes
our faith to its height. It's where we learn to trust outside
of sense or reason. For God does not always talk. He broods.
He retreats. He watches. He hides. He meddles. He probes.
And He is under no obligation to explain. Therefore, this
needful benediction to silence: *May your faith prove as strong.*
May your trust be nurtured in it. May your soul gather from
among its first fruits. May it be your best defense. May you find
instruction there. May the lessons of life unfold there.

In Christ, the warm Jesus within my silence, Amen

May you give a tongue to silence only when it asks for one.

911: It's Still a Call For Help. It's Just a Higher One.

Because of your love, save us.—Psalms 44:26 NCV

Will such a day ever be forgotten? Will not our calendars be marred forever with something dark and ugly, stillborn in this ninth month? We live in a world where security has allthe substance of a dream. On such a day, the hidden seams were loosed, the tight weave of our illusions began to unravel. Everything changed. In an instant, in an unforeseen moment, something was taken from us, something that will perhaps never be returned. The day of calamity is upon us. We will not talk it from us, with our best arguments. We will not reason it away, for our reason is flawed and earthly, in need of a redeemer. Madness has become the rule and not the exception. We can no longer trust in ourselves (as if we ever could). Love alone is remedy to this great dis-ease.

In Christ, the world's deep wound and its cure, Amen

In a day when it seems nothing and no one can be trusted, may love regather all your little trust in Him alone Who loves, Who *is* paying attention, Who *does* care, Who *is* worthy of our complete confidence.

911: It's Still a Call For Help. It's Just a Higher One. A Prayer

September 12

And in the shadow of Your wings I will make my refuge, until these calamities have passed by.—Psalms 57:1 NKJV

Lord, we did not know we had slept until the long dream had ended. We did not know we were afraid until the day proved indifferent to our defenses. The night too, and the stars, too scattered, too distant and aloof now to wish upon, like dull eyes, no longer seems to sparkle against our skies. Our illusions have failed us. We have deceived no one but ourselves. In sorrow, we confess this to You and stand before You penitent, yielded, desiring to put aside the madness that has ruled over us. O Love, swift and deliberate, make your descent and carry us upward and outward. Lift us beyond the reaches of our own folly. Gather us safe within your pinions, within the dark shelters of your wings and secret us away, set us upon a peaceful height, upon a high and holy place.

In Christ, my safe place, Amen

In a day of calamity, may fear have no allegiance in you, no consent, no fine print to entangle you.

LOVE AND THE HEROIC LIFE

But the LORD is with me as a mighty, awesome One. Therefore my persecutors will stumble, and will not prevail.—Jeremiah 20:11 NKJV

Only love can invoke the hero in you, call up the best that's in you in a moment of decision, stand Davids before giants unafraid. Only love can awaken the prince or rouse the sleeping princess in each of us, give you a cape or a crown, put within your gait the stride of royalty, with awe, mystery, and grace like an irresistible presence, like a flowing train to leave traces of you behind. *O Love, how bold, how regal, how original, how fresh, how delicate and how daring, how audacious and how gentle, how all-powerful, how holy, how fearful, and O, how rare.*

In Christ, *the invocation to heroism in me,*
the authority found in gentleness, the Sovereignty
in a single act of kindness, **Amen**

May you have a day to look back upon and to say that everything fit in its place, every intended thing and every little accident, that all things did and acted as they were meant to by some trick of inevitability, a day to wonder at, a day you can't remember being this good, a day upon which calamity had no claim, having no defense against your best.

September 14

And my God shall supply all your need according to His riches in glory by Christ Jesus. —Philippians 4:19 NKJV

Someone needs you today. Someone must ask no less than Christ of you. The little accidents of life, those happy accidents that quietly shepherd us outside our own order of things, those odd and lovely coincidences, may they find no resistance in you. May you be yielded beyond your common distractions, for love may lead by a different map than the one you studied at daybreak. For need is never still, never really quiet. It sends out its signals, its pulses, alarms. Some are obvious. Some are hidden. Some lay beneath all detectable thresholds. Some have no voice at all. *May all the hidden engines of sense within you be awake and vigilant, even as divinity on call.*

In Christ, *what this day will ask of me, Amen*

When you love, give them Christ or you give them nothing at all.

*And the ransomed of the LORD shall return, and come to Zion
with singing, with everlasting joy on their heads. They shall obtain
joy and gladness, and sorrow and sighing shall flee away.*
  —Isaiah 35:10 NKJV

*Lord, make what roads we travel on be safe. Post sentinels at
every bend, Your winged guardians along every stretch of unknown
highway. Let the passing of our time be sweet with company and
with the charm of simple conversation. Let the road hum its familiar
undersong. Let us drink deep the mystery of laughter. Let silence
be generous and easy, our meditations light and joyful. Let the hours
not give way to fatigue, weariness, or an overload of care, but sustain
us with expectation, with the promise waiting at the road's end.*

In Christ, *this day's fortunate road,* **Amen**

May you know your limits, those distant borders of yourself,
the lean outerworld where faith has little strength to feed,
where doubt and the unknown surround you like mist and
nightfall. Nonetheless, may you find Him there, your bright
God, in all His unexpected and yet welcomed presence, the
long arm of redemption.

My Portion

"The LORD is my portion," says my soul, "Therefore I hope in Him!"—Lamentations 3:24 NKJV

May some good thing, some outrageous and unexpected advantage, some liberal and immeasurable portion of good come to you. May it have the odd stamp of inevitability sealed within it. May it come labeled and with your name on it, impatient for you, by some express delivery, unstoppable in transit, blessedness with all your specifications, all the peculiar measures of you, that rescripts all your doubt and misbelief, that topples your little inner kingdom where dreams and longing in you have slept too deep and too long and thought things impossible.

In Christ, my excess, my famine, my good portion, Amen

May blessedness in you be generous, fluid, wild and unthinking, like nature unbound and ungoverned, a flood tide that comes with welcome upon a parched and joyless world.

BEHIND LOVE'S CURTAIN

He is the image of the invisible God, the firstborn over all creation.
—Colossians 1:15 NKJV

Go back in time a bit and think of those lunches neatly packed and brown paper sacked, well cookied and amply chipped, ziplocked and peanut buttered, that somehow magically appeared on the kitchen counter just before you went off to school in the morning. Or those crisp clean clothes, that by some miracle, were folded and put away in your drawers or in your closet. What fairy, what friendly and unseen phantom put them there? And there was mom, hidden behind love's curtain the whole time. We never even noticed. How could we? Love raised none of its own banners. It never does. It's difficult to draw attention to a self that has vanished.

In Christ, the love behind the curtain, Amen

And where is she now? Maybe she's consigned to memory. Maybe she's widowed and eats her meals alone, the good angel who watched over you in your youth, before you were given wings and rites of passage. *May love always be too young to forget.*

TILL YOU SEE YOURSELF

SEPTEMBER 18

*I opened my mouth and panted, for I longed for Your commandments.
Look upon me and be merciful to me, as Your custom is toward those
who love Your name.—Psalms 119:131-132 NKJV*

*Prevail over me, Lord. Conquer this little plot of mortality that
goes by my name. Wash me of myself, of all that is unneccesary
and unclean. Search my mystery till You see Yourself. You are my
deliverance, my liberation. You alone are the Exodus and I am
Egypt. You alone are my dawn, the day that breaks on all my
sleeping senses.*

Clothed and in my right mind, **Amen**

May you come to look into the mystery of God with a
maiden's sacred trust. Selfless, yielding and gentle. Soft as
down. A glorious martyrdom.

The Nexus

*For of Him and through Him and to Him are all things, to whom
be glory forever. Amen.*—*Romans 11:36 NKJV*

Love is the nexus, the binding cord, our link to all life and
to all time. Love illumines the deep trenches of memory
with an intense and searching light and urges sweetly back
again the Eden hidden in the blood. It's what love does. It is
the collective unconscious that we sought in our science of
the mind, in our attempts to explain our ancient connections,
when we began to dig at the roots.

**In Christ, my communion with all that has been,
all that is, and all that is to come, Amen**

May all time, past, present, and future dissolve into one heroic
and everpresent NOW.

LOVE IS PROPHETIC

"For the testimony of Jesus is the spirit of prophecy."
—Revelation 19:10 NKJV

Everything about Christ was alive. Everything He said. Everything He touched or that touched Him had the stuff of divine order in it. Nothing He did or said was out of place, too small, or insignificant. To be prophetic is simply for a thing to have this Christness about it, a strange mix of humanity and divinity. The prophetic word is the living word. Prophecy cannot fail any more than love can fail, no more than God can fail. And it's not limited to speech. It flows as well in action, making life itself a parable we can discern. It imposes Christ into what only appears at first to be coincidence or some happy accident. It gives the wholeness of life a voice. There is one message in prophecy and only one, and that is Christ and in Him it is always love.

In Christ, *the living testament that love proclaims in me, Amen*

May love be your stone of reckoning, your trusting inner prophet, the filter through which all considerations must pass, through which all your actions and reactions are first sifted, making your response singular, your oaths and commitments sure and soul deep, trusting love to the details.

LOVER'S LAMENT

For He satisfies the longing soul, and fills the hungry soul with goodness.—Psalms 107:9 NKJV

Lord, I do not understand much of this. Reason is overthrown. My assurances are deposed, cast down. My coverings have been stripped from me. My illusions are unstrung along with all I formerly believed to be true, no less unraveled, not to be fitted back again to hide my nakedness. All is consumed, scattered like ashes among the ruins of my former life. And love has done this. Love alone is answerable, guilty of this wondrous aggression imposed upon me. At last am I undone! What a lovely prayer that labors in me. And what a lovely God to make it sing.

**In Jesus, my sky that bends from pole to pole,
the Christ that covers me, Amen**

May you never fear the expectation of plenty, for the earth itself is but one of the spoils of the meek.

A Hidden Beam in the House of Love

In Him was life, and the life was the light of men.
   —John 1:4 NKJV

Let light in! Let it paint your house with brightness!
Let it rouse the bed where hope sleeps! Let illumination
prosper from ceiling to floor, from the tops to the laces,
from crown to keel! Throw back your curtains! Risk the
light! Risk the mounting day! Let love awaken your
twilit world with celebration, with invocations of light and
blessedness! *Take from me my popular myths and the arguments
they raise. Banish all my household gods, those that conspire against
You, that rage and murmur against the light. I will risk my soul
to love. Though I vanish. Though I am no more. Though I break
and splinter beneath the weight of kindness. I am but a servant
in the rule of charity, a hidden beam in the house of love.*

In Jesus, bright and beautiful, our illuminating Christ, Amen

May the Glory of God shine out from you, in audible
emanations, light disguised as words and as acts unmistakable
with beauty.

PRISONERS OF HOPE:
THE MYSTERY OF THE LOCKS

Return to the stronghold, you prisoners of hope. Even today I declare that I will restore double to you.—Zechariah 9:12 NKJV

Last night I visited a prison. It wasn't long before I realized how refreshing it felt to be there. What came over me was a sense of freedom that comes with an absence of pretension. There was a nakedness of spirit that the soul loves, a humility that invites God. There were no veils. None of these men could wear the disguises that we so readily wear on the 'outside.' All the uniforms were the same and we all knew why we were there. And God was there and with an ease so like Him, not so much in royalty, but closer, more intimate, more human, in His own stripes, the Jesus of Whom we talk. The only real difference between these inmates and too many of us is that *you could see their bars, you could see the thick and unfriendly doors that made prisoners of them.* The sound of their closing behind you touched your flesh with cold fingers. Still, there was something beautiful within the mystery of the locks.

In Christ, master of the locks, Amen

May love find the key of your prison-house and release you from any unnecessary restraints.

REFUGE

You are my hiding place; You shall preserve me from trouble; You shall surround me with songs of deliverance.—Psalms 32:7 NKJV

Each of us needs a refuge, a hiding place, a place we may burrow ourselves till trouble passes, a place where there is no shame in falling apart or in coming undone, a secret place, warm with light and stillness, where the soul may cease to toil, where we may recover what is lost or misused. But where there is no love, where there are only distortions of it, mimic and affectations of it, there is no sanctuary, and without sanctuary, loneliness itself becomes the source and hub of all our exchanges, inward and outward. Loneliness becomes no less than our vision of life. *Life is existence and nothing more.* And the reductions begin soon after. Something in the heart begins to wither and die. Love, or the lack of it, the phantom hope of it, turns inward, to a poison, takes what divine life there is and steals it from us and we have no recollection of the moment of departure. It leaves only ghosts. We are haunted by too many ghosts.

In Christ, light and stillness, my place to come inside, Amen

May you be a living sanctuary, a second home, warmed with the soft glow of familiarity, where a soul in need of a Sabbath may find one.

The Poet's Envy

And the Word became flesh and dwelt among us, and we beheld His glory, the glory as of the only begotten of the Father, full of grace and truth.—John 1:14 NKJV

You are the poet's envy, O Lord, for in You, love came to us like music, burned in us like fire, like a new and higher order of speech. It came without restraints in fluid and ceaseless procession, like a tide heaped upon its crest and dispersing itself. All things that gathered about You seemed to drift inward, inescapably inward, toward Your center, by some inescapable gravity. No one came into Your path unaffected or unmoved. We accepted or we rejected You. It was that plain before us. Some followed. Some fled. Some stopped up their ears. Some listened as if they heard music. But all knew the world had changed. For Your love, Your very presence was a reckoning, inescapable and relentless. Still is.

In Christ, love that came to us like music,
that burned in us like fire, **Amen**

May Christ be Master at the threshing floor where the heart drafts itself in speech.

THE GOD OF HAGARS AND HANNAHS, JOBS AND JONAHS

SEPTEMBER 26

God sets the lonely in families, he leads forth the prisoners with singing…—Psalms 68:6 NIV

There may be no greater loneliness than that felt by those living in the same household, who have become strangers. Maybe husband and wife living out time together, more like a sentence, having long reduced love to some vague dream or obligation, some relic of a past life, the ghost of something once true and tender that is no longer part of the exchange. In a silence too deep, in words too difficult, Absence prowls about the house, pillaging, plundering. And something beautiful is lost to the true wastes of time. *O God, let me not be so dull or indifferent to those closest to me. Give me the necessary radar that I may track warm life about me, that I may depose lonely from its height, from its seat of power, that I may be a friend to those You love, not just in posture or pretense, but even as Christ has befriended me.*

In Christ, the God of Hagars and Hannahs, Jobs and Jonahs, Amen

May you give elevations to life around you. May you be a means of access, a step, a ladder, a door, a passage, a corridor.

A Work in Progress

For we are His workmanship, created in Christ Jesus for good works, which God prepared beforehand that we should walk in them.
  —Ephesians 2:10 NKJV

Christ, make me as You are. Give me the assurances, that confidence, that rest in You that takes the toil from my life. And I would be free. Free to feel what I feel, to weep as long as I must, to laugh with all my strength, free to dance quietly alone or to sing in the company of the saints, free to fail without shame, free to win in my time, free to give to my last coin, to give away the very thing I am, that which I have sought for so long a time...my very self.

In Christ, the Word that gave a frame to nature itself, Amen

Even as the artist labors by a vision he keeps in his mind, may Christ's vision of 'you' dominate the ongoing procession of your life. You are a work in progress, life refinding itself.

YOU SAW STONE AND MORTAR

SEPTEMBER 28

As you come to him, the living Stone—rejected by men but chosen by God and precious to him—you also, like living stones, are being built into a spiritual house to be a holy priesthood, offering spiritual sacrifices acceptable to God through Jesus Christ. —1 Peter 2:4-5 NIV

Lord, You saw foundations, columns, and pillars in the place where we stood. When we considered our own worth no better than clay— brittle, useless, and unfashionable—You saw stone and mortar, the material of choice when it was time to build Yourself a house. When we were unsure of ourselves, when we knew little of what was in our own heart, when the testimony within us was still unrefined and unshaped, You drew poetry from our mouths. I am but a crude articulation of dust, awaiting the appointments of Him Who authors me, Who breathes life into nothingness, Who confounds the opinion of the world with acts of beauty and miracle. So come winds, scatter me as you are meant, as you are programmed, gather me up, take me where you will. I will not fear the elements that toss me about, nor Him Who commands them, Who harnesses the winds to useful service, Who has stilled the great storm in me to whispers.

In Christ, Author and First person, Creator and Craftsman, High Priest and Poemsmith, Amen

May love write new testimonies on the heart.

POVERTY: A CONDITION OF
THE SOUL IN LOVE

"Blessed are the poor in spirit, for theirs is the kingdom of heaven."
—*Matthew 5:3 NKJV*

Consider the beauty of a transparent morning. The sky sheer blue, as barren as the tongue for words to explain, an emptiness unspoiled and lovely. Consider the soul rid of its care, purged of its former identities, of its grey and lifeless counterfeits, like a cloudless sky. There is a poverty we need not fear, an emptiness the soul loves, a soul fitted and shaped for divinity alone. *O Sweet Oblivion, I am overcome with want, with the burden of neediness. I fear the loss of my illusions. I fear the poverty that would make me truly rich. My mind is thorns and stings, a confusion of branches. O, that I may leave my care among the lilies, that I may have certainty in my steps again, lightness and pleasance in my speech, and room within my spacious soul for no less than worlds to find shelter there.*

In Christ, my poverty, the great want in me, Amen

May you never fear when the heart aches in what it lacks. I would be suspicious of love that had no such wound.

HEART: THE CENTER OF COMMERCE

SEPTEMBER 30

The LORD is my strength and my shield; my heart trusted in Him, and I am helped…—Psalms 28:7 NKJV

There was less to think about then. Man and God were united by something greater than faith. Man did not yet labor to believe. There were no arguments to consider, no proofs to debate. Mind and heart were inseparable. Mind, the servant. Heart, the center of trade between deity and ourselves. But that order was overthrown and the heart became a casualty in the Rebellion, that unfortunate mutiny which resulted in the banishment of our father Adam and his Eve, that made them wanderers, pilgrims, laborers. Between heart and mind there was now a cleft, a chasm fixed that only love could cross. *Lord, heal this breach in me, this grievous fault, this old and unmended tear. That my heart and mind may live together again in absolute concord, in the order set down for them in the very beginning of things. That they may enjoy each other's company again. That I may rest in this hope that I cannot now explain. That when my mind is overwhelmed, when reason is overthrown, when intellect is bound in knots and tangles, my heart can trust. I am warm with possibility.*

In Christ, the curse's curse, Amen

May you trust even when reason says otherwise, when intellect has better arguments.

OCTOBER

Christ, the reign that softens the clay

October 1

Her children rise up and call her blessed; her husband also, and he praises her: "Many daughters have done well, but you excel them all."
  —*Proverbs 31:28-29 NKJV*

This is an actual note I found this morning in our kitchen, left in an obvious place where he would see it. Even with his teenage indifference and nonchalance, it will add something remarkable and irreplaceable to his day. Shad leaves for school at 6:45 AM. Benita left this note for him before that time. This is how love raises its voice in my house. And poetry is so easy for her. Hers is real, from an elevated place within her. I have to sweat for it, fat and breathless. (And I wondered why she got up so early! I thought it was the coffee.) The note read: *Shad, Good morning! I love you! Mommy.*

In Christ, the God so easy in her, the poetry so deep, Amen

Communion with God can be as close as a simple act, one that will remain warm with life and divinity long after the moment passes. May you discover within you the kindness of God, eager for expression and may He trust you with this grand commission.

ANOTHER GREAT FALL:
AN OCTOBER BENEDICTION

And He changes times and seasons…—Daniel 2:21 NKJV

May the warming of colors, leafy blots that dapple the earth,
that gild our banks, that weep scarlet upon our hills,
that jewel our dying lawns with gold and rubies,
our fields with blood and fire,
that set the earth ablaze in voiceless ecstasies,
in a conflagration of slow and heatless flames,
the transposing of the earth in its dying season,
may it invoke its sorrows to the heart,
called back from the deep reserves
like harvest and regathering, homecoming and reunion,
that may sweeten your day with remembrance of a forgotten time,
before ruddy and breathless youth was lost in our mirrors,
a time when our steps were lighter, quicker,
and there was something wild and untamed in them,
a time when mothers with rakes in their gloved hands,
with small talk in their mouths and strange hats upon their heads
burned the dried and doomed leaves in smoky mounds,
we were fascinated by the gossip in the flames
and the rising clouds that burned our eyes,
that filled our nostrils,
that delighted us with its pungent testimonies,
recalled now from the misty and smoke worn banks
with sudden assaults of awareness, thorns we tried to overstep,
some unaccounted loss that is strange and somehow wonderful,
that gnaws at the heart, that feeds at the root of life,
joy and grief feasting together
to a music for which no words can be written.

OCTOBER 3

That grace was given to us through Christ Jesus before time began…
—2 Timothy 1:9 NCV

Yesterday has no power over you. It must yield, even as tomorrow must yield. Unkind memory loses substance. There are no words, spells, no incantations of the mean and loveless whose bindings love cannot break, no fearful imagination love cannot put to flight. There are no walls high enough to keep love out, to hoard it, contain it, or tame it. No oceans deep enough to bury it, to silence it, to wash it from you. For once love is enthroned in the heart, time itself becomes as one of the conquered. *Its voice weakens. Its politics are stilled. Its influence and its privileges over you are lost.*

In Christ, Who calls time to account, Amen

May grace and mercy accompany you in your return to forgotten moments of your childhood, to daylight that lasted forever, to the napping afternoon, to that time when life began, when love took its first roots, when the world looked so large and we had eyes to match, when we were not afraid to be curious and spend whole days in amazement. We were artists then, without the burden of art. We learned our first lessons, some with pain, some with wonder. It was a time when believing was easy.

Be Remembered in Me

Remember those days in the past when you first learned the truth.
  —Hebrews 10:32 NCV

Creation itself was our first witness of You, Lord. It was inescapable.
The sun in golden arms warmed our young bodies with its parenting
light. We played and we napped among its beams. We were closer
to the earth then, to the grasses and to the animals that trafficked
our yards, that amazed us, that brightened our eyes with wonder as
we followed blindly their panting trails, as far as our fences would let
us. We were small. Untamed. Innocent. Our language was unformed,
primal, inarticulate, but our hearts were free and overflowed with
speech of its own, with life dispersing itself. We were not unaware of
You, for divinity was easier in us then, a big and bustling house. And
You spoke so clearly to us, in that ear we lose as we grow up. But be
remembered in me, Lord. And like a kiss, shy and selfless, that puts a
blush on the pale and reluctant cheek of doubting day, smooth the
wrinkle from this brow of care and father me hopeful into night.

In Christ, all that was lost refound, **Amen**

May all things of day seem strangely and by some wonder,
yours.

October 5

Be not deceived; God is not mocked: for whatsoever a man soweth, that shall he also reap.—Galatians 6:7 KJV

You have appointments. Some you've planned. Some will involve you without your consent. All things wait before you. Suspense accompanies the dawn, as sure as the sun. So ask yourself this: What do I bring to the day? Do I come anxious, catlike and suspicious, tiptoeing among the hours? Do I enter by bold strides? Am I the unwary fawn before the wolf? Or by the measure of good in me, can I enter with confidence, having laid my foundations, having sent out my invitations, having pollinated my world with love, with blessing, with mercy, with meekness, with honesty, as far as it is found in me, with grace, and so by these things and the authority within them give myself the right to live in the expectation of good, in the hope of a return that may come in an unsuspecting moment on my many investments? What a lovely choice. What precision in the scales. What a lovely God to impose such a law, such a canon of life.

In Christ, the precision in the scales, Amen

May you always consider well your invitations before you send them out.

DEATH, DISGUISED IN AUTUMN

For as in Adam all die, even so in Christ all shall be made alive.
  —*1 Corinthians 15:22 NKJV*

It's October. Death, disguised in Autumn, has come to us in a pageant of color, with limbs heavy and aflame, dappled with reds, yellows, and russets. Wonder returns, as it has, as it does, as it will, in the mellow dropping Fall, in the hiss and gossip of her branches. And the old man, Time, treads soft upon a cobble of leaves. For the earth again is yielding, bending to the burrowing winter and the afterlife, the April that is to come. *O, that I may not hesitate in love's simplest request of me, even at the surrender of my body, of my complete self, to be love's response to a single soul in want of it. I am love's supply. The bins ache with fullness. The branches, heavy with the spoils of time and the fruited season, with age and sweetness bend low to the earth in homage. It is the redeeming time.*

In Christ, my Afterlife, the April that is to come, Amen

May the thing for which you have co-labored with God and for so long a time, fashioned in a secret place by years and by a lifetime of hope, be realized at last. May the heart not sicken with delay. May your soul know its own season of harvest.

OCTOBER 7

I will not leave you nor forsake you.—*Joshua 1:5 NKJV*

Love is never alone. Ever.

In Christ, my everpresent God, Amen

When love requires a vow, may you put to death all other options. When it seeks a volunteer, may your hand be the first to rise.

INTERRUPTED

Lord, answer me because your love is so good. Because of your great kindness, turn to me.—Psalms 69:16 NCV

When my path seems too liquid and unsure, when I seem to be carried upon moving streams, having lost my familiar, solid and trusting pavements, when You are too much of a mystery to me, Lord, when I am too much of a mystery to myself, when the familiar becomes unfamiliar, when my mind seems banished from itself, when my eyes see strange things, when there is distance in those closest to me, when blankness eclipses the face of friendship and smiles recede, taking the last sweet wrinkle of mirth from our moments together, when I am lost and impossibly alone, when flight fills me and I am wingless, when my soul is bullied with suspense, when normal seems indifferent, when I am naked and fretful, when I fear the light of day and long for shadows to hide me, to comfort me in a place where I am faceless and no one asks my name, when prayers like this one say too much and leave no finishing mark, no punctuated end, for language itself is interrupted

Christ, when there is no period, no Amen, when the rule of prayer is overthrown, when protocol and formality is but a luxury, when they seem irrelevant, tasteless on the tongue of desperate man

May Christ alone be your soul's active and unending request.

OCTOBER 9

For if we live, we live to the Lord; and if we die, we die to the Lord. Therefore, whether we live or die, we are the Lord's.
—*Romans 14:8 NKJV*

Lord, I have been too comfortable with this me that's not quite me, this self-not-quite-myself-pretended-version of me. As if what I could be or what I refuse of myself is but an apparition that prowls among my shadows. I have settled for less, and therefore, by the law of love, have settled for nothing at all, consigning my soul to smallness. Until You, I did not know the difference. So let death claim that which is its own. Let it take from me that which by right belongs to it. That only what is deathless in me may remain. That life may break loose, gnaw itself free from the restraints. That life may find its full height. That life and love may come together in absolute harmony over me. That I may love even as love itself would be pleased. That I can be the me You first thought of, the Genesis me, the love that was Yours to die for.

In Christ, the love to die for, Amen

May the great discovery of your life be the discovery of yourself. Concerning this great adventure, may you be more the Columbus, not the Edison, the explorer and pioneer, not the inventor.

People, how long will you turn my honor into shame?
How long will you love what is false and look for new lies?
  —Psalms 4:2 NCV

If we deny love in the least measure of it, we deny it all. There's no way to circumnavigate that. Love too easily becomes a ghost among us, a distortion, an apparition, unsubstanced and lifeless. *Lord, deliver us from ourselves and from our loveless folly. Be the Good Physician that must rethink a broken limb if You must. Show our idols for what they are, as well as our reinventions of love. And have mercy, O God. Do not keep Your kindness from us. We have estranged ourselves to love and to each other. Love demands a bit more from us than we first suspected. So let love come upon us, like a sudden storm on an unsuspecting meadow. Let it take dominion over its own house.*

In Christ, the evidence of God's kindness to me, **Amen**

May love keep all appointments, complete all its assignments in you, the odd and the obvious, the grand and the commonplace.

Heavy Meddle

When I was a child, I spoke as a child, I understood as a child, I thought as a child…—1 Corinthians 13:11 NKJV

It seemed way too much for God to ask of anyone. Calamity and sorrow seemed to conspire against me. They were the wind and storm and I was the leaf. And in a moment, a kingdom toppled within me. I loitered in the dark among the ruins, a darkness that seemed to live, that crept about me, that kept me constrained within a small room with all my ghosts, with all my mirrors, and with all the black and savage cruelty of my sorrow. *But it was Christ Who washed me of my deceptions, of my myths, Who came to me in my pain and asked, "DO YOU LOVE ME?" My illusions alone were shattered, not the heart that had fed upon them. Through a knowledge bought with tears, He sought a truer fellowship, truer Oneness, truer kinship with me and trusted me enough, trusted His deposit of love within me enough to bring me to this point of overwhelm. It was Peter's betrayal all over again, Judas in my blood having its dark hour at last. It was an end that gave me a beginning.* Dear reader, I hope you understand.

In Christ, *my reckoning, my rebirth, Amen*

May Christ have all rights to you, access to your private self, the one you keep behind the veil.

LOVE AND TIME

For what is your life? It is even a vapor that appears for a little time and then vanishes away. —James 4:14 NKJV

When we were kids, we hardly noticed it. We lived for our distractions and for something that came to us in the eager light of morning. We were the true mystics. Without the burden of explanation. And we knew nothing yet of clocks. They were just faces on the wall, benign, funny, round. They said nothing we could understand. But all that changed as we got older. Those same faces took on a more stern appearance, more severe, almost religious. We stepped in formation to a new rhythm, the unnatural rhythm of ticking things, of alarms, schedules, mechanical life, without spontaneity. The droning day took something from us with each passing and put something colorless in our lives, consigning bold innocence to the memory of lost and unprofitable things. And we didn't see it coming. *Still, love overrules time and reconciles what is with what was, all in the hope of what will be.*

**In Christ, my access to what is timeless, Christ,
the hope of what will be, Amen**

May the divine and timeless within you be free to express itself. May love rule all your inward clocks.

CHRIST, MY CORRECTION

OCTOBER 13

Cleanse me from secret faults. Keep back Your servant also from presumptuous sins; let them not have dominion over me. Then I shall be blameless, and I shall be innocent of great transgression.
—Psalms 19:12-13 NKJV

I would rather stand in the white heat of Your rebuke, O Lord, than to be forgotten. Your correction is as sweet to me as my offense is bitter. So let the hidden forge blaze! Let love purge the excess from me! And let pardon thrive! Give defiance no refuge! Offer no place nor province, O God, for the dark man to hide. Quiet me now. I am warm with expectation.

In Christ, my correction, my good hope, my active rule, Amen

May correction be welcomed to the lover's soul, like form that sweetens in the eye of the artist, that liberates beauty and detail with every stroke of his brush, with every hard command of his hammer, or with the hiss of words under the poet's hand.

LOVE IS ON ITS WAY BACK

...Let us pursue the knowledge of the Lord. His going forth is established as the morning; He will come to us like the rain, like the latter and former rain to the earth.—Hosea 6:3 NKJV

Once upon a time, man understood eternity, for he understood love. Deeper than instinct, finer than thought, it was as simple as walks in the cool of day. He was at home with divinity. He did not have to study love. It was in the air. It was in the mists that watered the earth. It buzzed about the foliage and busied itself with trifles. The stars themselves were not silent, nor the sun and moon and all the elements. Leaves gave their greenness to the landscapes. They were ornaments of nature and not yet the odd fashion of man. Okay, we live in a different world now. *But let's dare to imagine that love is on its way back and live accordingly, that we may love as we were known to in a time before time, when eternity was easy.*

In Christ, the world come back again, Amen

May you grow in the discipline of love, master the fundamentals, learn the language, the limits, the necessary skills, the warm science, and the gentle art of it.

October 15

…And in the night His song shall be with me—a prayer to the God of my life.—Psalms 42:8 NKJV

Prayer: A solo flight. Inwardness rallying itself to words, words that none but heaven may hear. The genuine music of the soul. An unwinding of the great inner coil. A tongue given to need, to want, to the disquiet, a vent given to the heart warring against itself, a poetry assigned to all that lay silent and unsaid. The divine in each of us seeking itself in speech. The strange language of thanksgiving and desperation when mingled together. The stir of deep waters. *God looking into a mirror and asking it to explain what it sees.* A distillation of self before the Dread and Infinite. The one and perfect exchange with our one and lovely God. *Prayer is a lonely art. Then again, so is love.*

> **In Christ, my inwardness set to music, my God in the lonely hour, Amen**

May each day, from this day onward, have its own little history to look back upon, whose brief chronicle reads like a gospel, sings like music, arouses the ear like a parable or poetry, where time and timelessness kiss in one event, in one vocal uprising of the heart.

THE GREATEST OF GREATEST THINGS

But now abideth faith, hope, love, these three; and the greatest of these is love.—1 Corinthians 13:13 ASV

Faith, to pilot my soul on this dim planet. Faith, my eyes when I cannot see the path before me. Faith, when mystery is too much for me, when life refuses to explain itself. And hope, to sustain me in an unsure time. Hope, when faith weakens in me. Hope, when believing has labored too hard, grows silent and pale. But so much more than these provisions, love alone lets me partake of You, Lord. Love is my Eucharist, the taste of God for my hunger. Love, no less than life itself to me, divinity in the midst of me, God in my middlemost parts. Love, when faith and hope, my twin guides, have run their limits. And if I be spent, if I be Your coin of exchange in this soiled world, if I lose myself, vanish in the majesty of a simple act, may it be in love, the greatest of greatest things.

In Christ, *no less than life itself to me,* **Amen**

May you explore life with the awe of a child, the zeal of a holy man.

GIVE UP THE GHOST!

OCTOBER 17

Lead me in Your truth and teach me, for You are the God of my salvation; on You I wait all the day.—Psalms 25:5 NKJV

If I wear a mask and you wear a mask, we meet, we interact, and wish to exchange even some small part of ourselves, what happens? Nothing much. It's no more than one plastic form engaging with another. Authenticity is hidden in deception. Our encounter is but spin, a slight of hand, a mere phantom hope of a person and not the person themselves, roles being played, a ghost encounter, with empty, ghostlike results. All that can follow is a pretense of amity, a pretended harmony that cannot help but give way to suspicion, contention, argument, and exile. *Let us take the work out of our exchanges with each other.* Do not mock love, or life, with some colorful invention of yourself. Love delights in truth and serves best the exposed, the unguarded, and the innocent who live by that truth. Love offers no options.

**In Christ, Who gave up the ghost, Who came
back to us in Glory, Amen**

May others look to you as one looks into a mirror and may they be amazed at what is reflected there, in what they see in themselves.

When the Groans of Earth
Reached Heaven High

But he gave up his place with God and made himself nothing.
—*Philippians 2:7 NCV*

God divested Himself of majesty and came to us, became visible to us though we knew Him not nor suspected it not, became even as one of us, ordinary, indistinguishable, neither above nor beneath, but in the middlemost of us. Love gave itself no choice. I don't think it could. *When the groans of earth reached heaven high, Christ was the response.* Love asks the same of you and I. An emptying. A divestment. A reversing of the process by which gods are made in this world. A descent. A dethroning. An uncrowning. An unmaking. And yet what a lovely paradox. For in this Christ-sufficient life, in this grand submission, we find ourselves at last and among what we thought were but ruins.

In Christ, my soul at liberty, given wings and rights to the wind, Amen

When love asks you to divest yourself of human glory, when it asks you to descend from your high places, or to empty your stores on its behalf and leaves you with nothing, no trace of your former greatness, may the soul understand, yielding reverently, bowing sweetly, rejoicing tearfully, before her conqueror and king.

OCTOBER 19

But those who wait on the LORD shall renew their strength; they shall mount up with wings like eagles, they shall run and not be weary, they shall walk and not faint.—Isaiah 40:31 NKJV

HOPE, like remedy in the blood, a wholesome medicine, an antidote, a countermeasure against all the infectious harms and contaminations of this world. *HOPE,* to sustain us when the days are lean and dreams are faint for lack of feeding. *HOPE,* diamond-bitted *HOPE,* that mines beneath all our hardened surfaces where promise lay sleeping too long, too silent, and too deep. *HOPE,* whose youthful eye still sees something grand in the dull and doubting day. *HOPE,* that joy may feed upon. *HOPE,* wonder that puts Christmas and all good seasons back into the calendars of the heart. *Lord, I live, therefore I HOPE. Give HOPE its assignments over me, even as I yield to the love that gives it life and sense.*

In Christ, all I can tell you of HOPE, Amen

May hope be nurse to those things yet to be realized in you, those deep seedlings planted of God.

ANOTHER RULES HERE!

But when perfection comes, the things that are not perfect will end.
—1 Corinthians 13:10 NCV

Love shapes and reshapes us, fashions us in its own
likeness, processes us through its own seasons and schedules,
takes from us what is incompatible to itself, and makes
its habitation within us a hallowed place. And though this
pilgrimage may begin at birth (for I do not know), it does
not end at death, for death is just a mark, another entry
in love's great diary. *So lead me, Lord, by the way that I would
not take. Take me by that hand I had refused to give you. Be the
path that I denied to walk. Command my heart, this mismanaged,
idling heart, that I may say, "Another rules here!" I am in process.
So come, you blessed seasons, weather yourself upon me, blast me in
your furnaces, blow me about in your winds, warm me beneath your
suns, chill me to the bones with your lean winters, till Christ be
satisfied in me.*

In Christ, the reign that softens the clay, Amen

May you be ever pliable, fixable, teachable, moldable, pliant,
stretchable.

LOVE THAT MAKES EVEN DEATH LOOK GOOD

OCTOBER 21

Now if we died with Christ, we believe that we shall also live with Him, knowing that Christ, having been raised from the dead, dies no more. Death no longer has dominion over Him.
  —Romans 6:8-9 NKJV

O Immortal Love, most uncommon God, Love that redeems time, Love that puts to silence the abuse, the injury, the injustice of a cruel and unforgiving past, Love that renders death powerless and time voiceless as stone. Rewrite the diary my heart has kept. Let my soul be overcome with wonder, till I am mute with awe, till I be senseless with joy, till something wild and jubilant, like daybreak sweeps over me.

In Christ, *love that makes even death look good,* **Amen**

May death have no power to silence joy. May grief and loss be reconciled to her. May joy rise magnificent in the midst of them, putting their powers in rightful place and proportions in the heart, and with her own tears, wash it clean, absolving and purifying it, giving sorrow a beauty only she can give to it. For true joy is deeper than happy, more majestic than death.

What do Five Loaves, Two Fish, and a Cruse of Oil Have to do With Love?

So they all ate and were filled, and they took up twelve baskets full of the fragments that remained.—Matthew 14:20 NKJV

What do five loaves, two fish, and a cruse of oil have to do with love? Supply. Inexhaustible supply. *Love cannot be emptied of itself any more than God could cease to exist.* It's the way of the infinite and the timeless. Think of fingerprints, snowflakes, and the unrepeatable YOU. God never gets bored. There's too many of us.

In Christ, my supply, my plenty, Amen

May you live a life as God designed it, a life that makes sacred the humblest portions of it, a life in ascent, set apart, a Christ-sufficient life, sealed in divinity, selfless, yielded, broken, even as redeemers and healers are broken, a life lived in love, as if heaven, eternity wide and timeless deep, yet as close, familiar and unnoticed as your next breath, is in endless pursuit of all your hours.

OCTOBER 23

"For with God nothing will be impossible."—Luke 1:37 NKJV

During this season, we reset our clocks. We get to push time backwards and sadly that's as close as some of us will ever come in the participation of a divine act. The push of a few buttons, a few cranks on an old clock and it's done. Too many think we can just as easily manipulate love, as if love itself can be altered at the push of a few buttons, at the crank of a few well-programmed clichés. Love is *other* than us, divine, immutable, and no more than God can divest Himself of Himself, can love be anything other than what it is. Divinity is a sure thing in this world and seeks its own. *Therefore, love is not an impossibility for you nor is it an unwilling teacher, but love must have its own way. Everything in you may scream in defiance. You may howl at the October moon. You may bark at a passing car. You may break down. For love is conquest, Christ the conqueror, You it's prize.*

In Christ, when love was more than possible for me, Amen

May life be found where no life was possible. May that which is barren in you become a birthing place, your wilderness a fruited grove. May hidden streams and mists water your fields.

MEET THE BITTERSAULS

I will say of the LORD, "He is my refuge and my fortress; My God, in Him I will trust." Surely He shall deliver you from the snare of the fowler and from the perilous pestilence.—Psalms 91:2-3 NKJV

Meet the Bittersauls! That loud, ill-mannered family of petty feeders and negotiators, who, by some inclination in their blood, by some miscalculation of nature, can jar you out of your peace, rattle you, shoo calm and comfort right from you. They seem to haunt your space with their own disquiet. Yet, when they wear you down and when you know no option but flight, there is a secret place you may take refuge, where you may lose yourself for a needful time within His shadow, in that Adullam hidden from the world, that stronghold of kings and castaways, where psalms and sovereigns are shaped and with all the consent of heaven, a quiet place where the Davids of this world may come to themselves again and regather their strength. *O, those wacky Bittersauls! They lead us to the Lord in such strange and compelling ways. God bless 'em! God bless 'em all!*

In Christ, my Adullam, my hideaway, my regathering, Amen

May love make you a poet, a warrior, a prince, calling out a David from among all the bitter, broken, and uncrowned Sauls.

A Cautionary Tale

October 25

My soul waits for the Lord more than those who watch for the morning—
Yes, more than those who watch for the morning.—Psalms 130:6 NKJV

We are a world of watchers. The eyes, once the windows
to the soul, or so the poets tell us, have become petty feeders
among the senses, insatiate, having lost the good light. And
these anxious and 911-weary times have heaped upon us even
more watching and at a higher pitch. Caution has bound us
in reds, yellows, and shades in between. Strange fashion for
a civilized world. It's a dizzy world, a world of spin, of devices,
a world of overthrow and intrigues, a world of veils and
counterfeits, of multiple gods, a world peopled with impostors
and pretenders, religious charlatans, a world enamored of its
own image. But let me turn this cautionary tale to benediction,
and put love back in the mouth of this sad little catechism.

In Christ, my wellness in a world so ill at ease, Amen

May Christ be the nexus that binds you to all things fine and
worthy, as well as to the lowly and the unloved, to all warm
humanity and the divinity beneath its veil, to all things holy,
peaceful, and otherworldly, to all things good and true, just
and honorable.

GLOBAL WARMING—A PRAYER

Lord, your love fills the earth. Teach me your demands.
—Psalms 119:64 NCV

Let me not hoard myself today or be afraid of losing that which is not mine to lose, the earth and our little plots of it, our treasured acres, those small allotments that we dress, that we manicure, that we lay our fences round, of which we say 'mine.' We are here for a brief visitation, a small and lonely season. And that itself is a gift. The best that will be said of me is that I LOVED, that I gave warmth to the world as it gathered itself to me. Let my epitaph so read. For love is my tribute to You for the remaining days of my life, Lord, my worship, my sacrifice, this living martyrdom set adrift within me. I am grateful. I am yielded. And I love you. You amazing, unsettling God.

In Christ, my earth, my one, true, and good possession, **Amen**

May you begin to love as if these hours were the last given to you, as if tomorrow was not on the calendar.

It Begins With Coffee

October 27

The end of a thing is better than its beginning…
   —Ecclesiastes 7:8 NKJV

It begins with coffee. Then I will putter around my desk and may go through the 'mystery' pile. Lighting a candle helps, and perhaps music, usually soft and voiceless. All this before one word is written. Sounds like romance doesn't it? I think maybe it is. It's a ritual I seem to go through before I actually get to the work, kind of a mnemonic device that helps something to awaken in me. I'm usually here before dawn. There is something cool about being here before the light, while my house is quiet and sleeping. When I first met the love of my life, Benita, the first time we actually sat together, it was over a cup of coffee. She liked hers the way I liked mine (a confirmation, set like the stars). Our first conversation was electric with adventure, caffeine, adrenaline, and other exciting things. But it was love that sweetened our cup, the 20 years, the two kids, and the life that has followed bravely after.

In Christ, the cup of life, love's deep drink, Amen

May love entrust to you its mighty heart.

The Martyrdom Requested of Me

For you were bought at a price; therefore glorify God in your body and in your spirit, which are God's.—1 Corinthians 6:20 NKJV

I will not seek it, Lord, and yet I will not refuse it. I will not fear it when it comes, for I die daily if love is served in me. In love, I live just outside myself, in an elevated place, in that Christ-place just between heaven and earth. And though it takes one death, one sure surrender to get there, death itself has no government, no voice over me. Ambition, desire, hunger, and all the other considerations as these are but memories of once relevant things. You are my confidence. You are my indifference to things that once owned me. You are my weakness and my strength. You are my deep wound even as You are the medicine in my blood. You are all that I have misunderstood. You are all I long to know. You have estranged me from my own native earth. You have set new oaths, new vows on my lips. You are the martyrdom that love has requested of me. This took years to understand, for I held so tightly and hoarded my little life and regarded it as my own.

In Jesus, *the martyrdom requested of me,* **Amen**

May love have another inch of ground upon your little plot of earth.

THAT'S ENTERTAINMENT

With her enticing speech she caused him to yield, with her flattering lips she seduced him.—*Proverbs 7:21 NKJV*

Entertainment is everything today. Image and posturing rule, perceptual architecturing, the art of making believers and feeders of millions, all to appease the twin gods: Gain and Glory. We've all been contaminated and immunity is difficult to come by. But love will outlast all its saboteurs and detractors, all the enchantments of this glittering world, those within and those outside its own camp. Love is not the delicate flower poets would have us believe, nor is it so easily withered in the heat of our appetites. It is unshakeable, more than the earth itself. *Love is too much Christ to be otherwise.*

In Christ, my immunity, my gathering ground,
all that is truth and beauty, Christ, my eyes redeemed,
my soul washed, my mind delivered, Amen

May your mind be cleared of meddlesome debris, of things that have no business, no further trade among your thoughts.

TIME HEALS NOTHING

Heal me, O LORD, and I shall be healed; save me, and I shall be saved, for You are my praise. —Jeremiah 17:14 NKJV

Time heals all wounds. It's one of our oldest myths. It has the seal of antiquity and common use upon it. We employ it with the weight of a proverb. It just doesn't happen to be true. Time takes on the appearance of medicine, but it has no such properties. It's an opiate. It allows a grief or a wound to settle beneath our surfaces, to sleep or to hush itself, but *time heals nothing.* It's only time. Love is the healer. Love is the great medicine that binds our wounds. Okay, some of you will say, *"You've taken this love thing too far!"* My response, *"O, I do hope so!"*

In Christ, Adam's physician, the medicine of earth, Amen

May love take you farther than you have previously tolerated, to the very limits of yourself and then some, where your myths, your fables, and all the fictions that have sustained you up to now become ineffective.

Until the Day Breaks and
the Shadows Flee

October 31

Jesus Christ is the same yesterday, today, and forever.
    —Hebrews 13:8 NKJV

Love is where heaven and earth find a common citizenry
between them. And love is no different in this world than
it is in the next. When the curtain is pulled back at last,
love will not suddenly change as if to become something
else, any more than God will. *We will see then only what we
refuse now.* Life is happening to you and I at full pitch, and
we will be spent of mortality soon enough. Therefore, love!
Heaven is just that close. Watch and love! There are signs
of morning. It'll be daybreak soon enough.

> ***In Christ,*** *love here and hereafter, the olive branch*
> *between the two,* ***Amen***

May the heaven in you, love in residence, be easily accessible
to a world that only dreams of one.

NOVEMBER

Christ, my assessment of all things,
the reply I give to life

NOVEMBER 1

"Yes, I swore an oath to you and entered into a covenant with you, and you became Mine," says the Lord God.—*Ezekiel 16:8 NKJV*

May your love have all the right stuff, all the right measures and proportions of divinity and humanity, all the Jesus mortality can bear. May your whole frame be set by His standard, His own flawless architectures. May your mind and the things that occupy it, all your assessments and all your judgments be sufficient with light and divinity, filtered, sifted in Christ. May your love endure all hazards and all common obstacles, seen and unseen, within and without. And may your love have Christ enough to endure strong mortality and all the hard fates of this brief and beautiful life, Christ enough to withstand all the delights and distractions of this world.

In Christ, what it takes to love, Amen

May your love have Christ enough to last.

But clothe yourselves with the Lord Jesus Christ...
  —*Romans 13:14 NCV*

Christ, when my tongue is still at last, Christ, when the night is restless and uneasy, Christ, when my soul is wingless and too heavy for flight, Christ, when I am spent, when Heaven must come to me, Christ, when words are but folly, Christ, the mirror, the David I seek among the kings of the earth, Christ, this madness, this joy, this Zion celebrated in my blood, Christ, the AMEN at the end of all words, when peace puts a period to my lament.

In Christ, where deity and desire conceive in me, Amen

May Christ alone be the substance of things hoped for, that makes faith worth the one life you've invested to attain it.

NOVEMBER 3

"Holy, holy, holy, Lord God Almighty, Who was and is and is to come!"—Revelation 4:8 NKJV

Thank You, Lord, for this bright new order of things, the older one but days, memories, and one life behind me now, consigned forever with the faded image of my former self. Thank You for the resetting of all inward clocks, for putting to silence the menace of time, that dark overlord, who kept my soul bound by the strength of his second hand, whose music to me was but discord and dissonance. For every step forward, however brief, however unsteady or unsure, at whatever cost to me, is an age, an epoch, a beginning, a rebirth. You have put wonder back in the day and mingled the hours, these moments we have, with the Tomorrows still to come and the Always we but dream of, that distant and single light we hope by. All this by a promise that only love can keep.

In Christ, the promise love kept, Amen

May time be a friend to you.

PATMOS: WHEN GOD WOULD HAVE YOU TO HIMSELF ALONE

Where has your beloved turned aside, that we may seek him with you?—Song of Solomon 6:1 NKJV

The Gospel *in* John was like anarchy in his blood, like a thunderstorm, glorious, wild and out of control, and too much for the ruling authorities, so he was consigned to this remote place. Patmos would complete his pilgrimage, end his days, and live up to its odd name[13]. But here the great door opens for him. Beyond Patmos we hear little of the old man. Our Bible ends there too, in a revelation. In this lonely place, love entrusted itself to him completely, unwrapped, stripped of its darker, more obscure coverings and in a time of exile, of banishment, of loneliness, at the end of life as he ha known it. *Love is strange that way. And so consistent.*

In Christ, the full account, the gospel in John, Amen

May love show itself to you at last in all its hidden splendor, in your own Patmos, when self is quiet, when surrender in you has done its good work, when you are weary of mortality, when God would have you to Himself alone.

---

13 Patmos – 'My killing' (Greek)

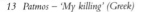

NOVEMBER 5

That which is has already been, and what is to be has already been; and God requires an account of what is past.—Ecclesiastes 3:15 NKJV

Most of us nurse some form of regret, some form of *'I wish I could go back and change things.'* or *'I wish I'd never said that or done that.'* Maybe it was neglect. Maybe it was a wound inflicted upon someone, deliberately or perhaps without your awareness, some offense of a long forgotten and indifferent time, a crime of youth and complicated passions. You may even ask yourself, *'How could that be me? Who was that person?'* You know it's different now, but you can't call back those things. Still, love can redeem the time. *More overpowering and more tenacious than regret, wiser than our grief, love is a liberator. It has mastery over offence, over death, and time. Love is an olive branch between you and your own soul, between what is and what has been. It closes the distance between you and your peace.*

In Christ, our so very Now, so very redeeming God, Amen

May you know what it means to live responsibly and yet in the moment, for love will not behave according to your plans and schedules, nor to any reason you may apply to it. It will not be plotted, charted, or mapped. Love's essence is divine, therefore it is timeless and submits to no clock and to no reason but its own.

The secret things belong to the LORD our God...
   —Deuteronomy 29:29 NKJV

May Christ find the door to your secret life, within the thickets, within the deep riddle of you, the hidden life that we keep to ourselves, the one we suffer alone. May you leave a trail of crumbs. May He be the tampering, meddlesome God, the God Who loves and Who saves still, the God Who will not leave you to the will of dark and reckless imagination nor to the menace of things unseen. May He Who loves, love like the God you suspect Him to be, filling with Himself the very finite ends of your little earth. May He Who is the God of Peace, be the very peace you make with yourself.

In Christ, *the code that unsecrets my life,* **Amen**

May Christ redeem you from your own darkness, from some private tyranny that overshadows the heart. May He save you from you.

November 7

For He will deliver the needy when he cries, the poor also, and him who has no helper.—Psalms 72:12 NKJV

I think this is what I may like about Him the most, that He is God not just upon my pleasant heights, but in my depths as well, God at the frayed ends, in the lonely recesses. He is a frontiersman, Who sought us in our own wilderness, when we were caught in the thickets of our own dark wood, Who came to us before we knew to call. He is a mender, particularly of those articles of His own original design, those marvels of clay and complication. And He still works the seams of this threadbare world. He is still God at the margins, where the unloved steal about in shadows, in but the forms and relics of men. He is still Father to the lost and unfriended, the exiled and the desperate, those who stand outside the common circles of life. *He is a lover, first and always.*

In Christ, the late Adam, the worker of clay, Amen

May Christ find no resistance in you when He sets your soul upon His wheel. May your clay be soft. May it conform to no shape but that which He gives it.

When We Touch:
A Sacred Conversation

"Somebody touched Me, for I perceived power going out from Me."
—Luke 8:46 NKJV

He could manage only the smallest groans. A Sister of Charity[14] leaned over him in his railed bed and began to stroke his chest. Because of the resistance she felt beneath her hand, the strokes were firm and confident. It wasn't just tenderness. It had more in it than that. He lay in a coil, tightly wound and she was his angel of release. Slowly the wildness, the lost and uncontrollable thing within him began to calm, to cease its endless struggle with itself. The coil began to unwind. Limbs, once dwarfed with tightness began to loosen their restraints. His face, once taut and disfigured, began to soften, to form into the trusting and ruddy face of a small boy. His breathing slowed to long and tranquil waves. Their eyes were fixed on one another. And there were no words, only something sacred between them, a primal dialogue that had no tongue. *O, this Wondrous authority of touch! Wordless divinity dispersing itself through the hands!*

In Jesus, *tender and touchable, Love with hands, Amen*

May tenderness be found in you in a world afraid to touch, a world sterilizing itself.

---

14 *Order established by Mother Teresa of Calcutta*

WHEN WE TOUCH: A SACRED CONVERSATION—A PRAYER

NOVEMBER 9

"Thomas, because you have seen Me, you have believed. Blessed are those who have not seen and yet have believed."
   —John 20:29 NKJV

You could no longer touch us. You were lifted just high enough that we could no longer touch You. The heavens turned dark and brooding. Clouds quarreled above us with blasts of thunder and shocks of electric and opposing fire. The earth cried in violence, in tempests, and heat. Skies wept bitterly. For love lay hushed upon a crude wooden beam. Three days and an eternity later, the sun came out again, but we were still tear-deep in slumbers. When we awoke, we thought we saw you on the shore. We jumped from our boats, naked and wild, for we were freed from our nets. At Your command, we touched Your wounds and believed. The twin-minded Thomas in me cried out, "My Lord and my God." May I never overlook the prayer liberated in a human touch, a prayer larger than words, deeper than the deepest groans, warmer than life.

In Jesus, warm to the touch, the Christ that disperses through my hands, Amen

May love be your strong countermeasure, your vaccine, the antidote against toxic unbelief.

But You, O LORD, do not be far from me; O My Strength, hasten to help me!—Psalms 22:19 NKJV

If I am sick, in need of a healer, if I am diseased, in need of medicine I cannot afford, if I am broken on the hard stone of my own denials, Lord, may You alone be the Armageddon that will decide my end, the great and final contest that will determine what is to become of me. You are the reckoning day of my spirit, a spirit that wishes itself free, a spirit that takes this risk to speak. My soul can but weep when it remembers wings and its former flight. But let this prayer in me resolve itself to this: If anyone would come after me, let it be Him alone…

Christ, my day of reckoning, Christ, the long arm of redemption, Christ, my comfort, Christ, humility if it takes in me at all, Christ, my dream if I sleep, Christ, the heaven when I awake at last, Christ, the sought after Amen

May Christ be your hidden and unexpected opportunity, your good fortune in an unfortunate time.

A Song in the Mouth of an Angel

November 11

For mine eyes have seen thy salvation, which thou hast prepared before the face of all people; a light to lighten the Gentiles, and the glory of thy people Israel.—Luke 2:30-32 KJV

Thank You, Lord, for this salvation that continues minute by gathering minute, that mounts up day by glorious day, for this love that overthrows me, that clarifies my world, that tells me who I am, that offers me up so freely, this love that turns my dull and lifeless prose to poetry, that confers upon me uniqueness, that gives music, shape, and distinction to my odd and lovely form. O, that my name should come to Him like a song in the mouth of an angel, as lovely as truth in the mouth of innocence.

In Christ, my unrelenting Savior, my jealous God, Amen

And that which is virginal, unexplored, reserved, untouched, unspoiled, hidden beneath your cluster of veils, may it awaken, may it speak with its first voice, see with its first joy of sense, sing with its first note of gratitude, touch with its first evidence of warmth and set the eyes of your curious world to admiration.

Thank You! Why? I Don't Know.

"The Lord GOD has given me the tongue of the learned, that I should know how to speak a word in season to him who is weary. He awakens me morning by morning, He awakens my ear to hear as the learned."—Isaiah 50:4 NKJV

Because love puts responsibility back in the speech, the following are just a few items that should be kept in good supply, well rehearsed and ready for employment. *"THANK YOU."* More than etiquette, it puts nobility in our exchanges, an ornament of grace to the tongue. It's a softening word. It opens gates and builds bridges. Quite the little architect, this one. *"WHY?"* It's a healthy word, a probing, tampering, meddling word, better used in sincerity than in defiance. It may debate within the heart, till faith says "Enough!" till faith puts to silence and irrelevance all questions. Finally, to say *"I don't know"* is to simply say you have no answer, that you are free enough, vulnerable, honest, and transparent enough to reply in such a way that reveals a soul at peace with itself, which is always a great response, and a refreshing one. *But what do I know? Ask your Father!*

In Christ, *the light by which I search my soul for words,* **Amen**

May your mouth be like the gate of heaven where only the righteous may pass.

THE WATCH I KEEP

NOVEMBER 13

My love will watch over him forever, and My agreement with him will never end.—Psalms 89:28 NCV

O, that I may walk and carry myself gently before love, that I would be a faithful watcher at love's gate, listening for its voice, discerning its face in a crowd, knowing when it stirs within and about me, that I may be proven love's worthy host. And may I never fear to love or to lose all that I have for the smallest measure of it. May fear have no voice at all, no politics in the heart. Let me not waste this freedom, but rather let me spend myself only on those things worthy of Him, that bring joy to the heart of Him, Him Whose love has the rule and governing in my blood.

In Christ, the watch I keep, **Amen**

May you live in the same suspense as lovers do, in eager expectation of His appearing.

No one has power over the spirit to retain the spirit, and no one has power in the day of death.—Ecclesiastes 8:8 NKJV

Because love has the stuff of forever in it, we may enjoy eternity in the present. And though love renders time mute, it makes the moments we have, even the most insignificant of them sacred, for *we are answerable to the divinity within those moments.* Each brings with it its own opportunity for love. Like a good angel ascending and descending the ladder between heaven and earth, divinity and humanity, between time and timelessness, love has charge in both domains, and makes the two one, allowing you and I to partake of heaven on the dullest of days, in the most unsuspecting time.

In Christ, *the salvation of a single moment, Who, like the stars, calls them each by name,* **Amen**

May you do all that love asks of you in the moment, like a good servant who knows his master's mind after so long a time in his presence.

NO OPINION BUT CHRIST

Why do the nations rage, And the people plot a vain thing?
—Psalms 2:1 NKJV

These are days of suspense, days when the great experiment
of man is tested, days of nations and news, of treachery
and heroism, of lawlessness and other mischiefs. War, like an
iron man, visits our TV dens, inhabits our spaces, like a dark
spectacle, a dream acted out just a few steps from us, and still
we think it beyond ourselves, in a remote part of a world
far beyond the safe closure of our walls. But we are not free
of him. And he is not a dream. *We live in a world brought to
hazard by its own poisons. Still, I will take the risk of love. I have
no opinion but Christ.*

> **In Christ, *my assessment of all things,**
> **the reply I give to life, Amen***

May His command to love have first voice in the discipline
that rules you, first seat in the congress that governs you.

IT JUST CAN'T BE THIS MUCH WORK

You search the Scriptures, for in them you think you have eternal life; and these are they which testify of Me. But you are not willing to come to Me that you may have life.—John 5:39-40 NKJV

When I first believed, I sought truth from every possible and reasonable source (although I was little concerned with reason as most lovers must admit). I was wild with feeding. I fed on everything, anything, it didn't matter. But love changed all that, claimed me for its own and put an end to the madness. By some awareness I can't explain, I knew *surrender* was what I had overlooked. That done, love and life began to come together in a concord I had to call *Christianity*. All the rest of it, all I had thought was love and faithfulness now seemed way too much work. Love showed itself easier than that. What is difficult is the untraining, the rethinking ourselves back to holiness again, back to love again. I'm not even sure we can pull this off. But love can.

In Christ, *love uncomplicated, life without webs,* **Amen**

May wonder return to you again, wonder that makes faith such little work.

COMMITTED TO THE DUST

NOVEMBER 17

But Jesus bent over and started writing on the ground with his finger.—John 8:6 NCV

As a writer, it's difficult to imagine saying the things Christ said and not committing them to paper, Who instead committed His words to the dust and to the inky chronicles of a few guys who smelled like fish. *Only God could trust like that. Only love could be so certain.* His was a new message, that dazzled our sense, that maddened us with joy, like sunlight on moving waters, so alive, so eager with truth, a gospel so divine and unstoppable, and still, His tablet of choice was the dust, soft, compliant dust, that could be moved by no more than a whisper, become legible at the slightest bidding of His touch. His preferences have not changed.

**In Him Who turned the dust to stones
to build Himself a house, Amen**

May love weave wonder into words. May it give a voice to psalms yet unwritten, to things that brood sweetly about the heart.

BLESSEDNESS

Blessed is the man who listens to me, watching daily at my gates, waiting at the posts of my doors.—Proverbs 8:34 NKJV

Blessedness is an imprint, a living seal, an endowment, an impartation, a sharing of the Divine. It's not a thing that we can readily give ourselves. It's an elevation, a removal of distance between your heart and His. Blessedness is also a defense, a shield against the indifference, the apathy, the treachery, against all the cunning devices of this plotting world. Blessedness outfaces calamity and misfortune, allowing them no politics in the heart. Exemption from trial is not bound in a promise, but blessedness in the very midst of it is. And perhaps that's where it does its finest work and gives us the evidences we need, that God is still in the midst of things, even when life moves along at its own erratic pitch.

In Christ, our blessedness, our inward happy, Amen

May joy find a place of permanence in your soul. May it have the seal of authenticity, stronger than imagination or invention. May it rise without impediments, unstoppable, even as an eagle takes flight, majestic to behold upon its heights.

To the Maker of Lovers
and Holy Men

November 19

When You said, "Seek My face," my heart said to You, "Your face, LORD, I will seek."—Psalms 27:8 NKJV

I want to be a holy man, to enjoy that life which only love can purchase for me, to know the joy of innocence again, so bright, so engaging, and so alive, innocence that lives by a faith it little thinks of. I want to be fearless. And free. I want love alone to pilot me, to shepherd me as life gathers me to itself. I want to trust God for the redemption of each day that remains to me. I want miracle to be at home with me, for wonder to play as easy on my tongue. I want to trust the mystery before me, to know that sweet anticipation known to none but lovers, the foretaste of wonders yet to come.

In Christ, the Maker of lovers and holy men, Amen

May holiness define you when the world seeks an explanation. May it be easily remembered on that day when the books are opened and the chronicles are read. May angels weep to themselves for the beauty of the music written there.

Worship Ascending

Take away from Me the noise of your songs, for I will not hear the melody of your stringed instruments. But let justice run down like water, and righteousness like a mighty stream.
—Amos 5:23-24 NKJV

O, that worship would break free of the limitations we impose upon it! That it would rise as it was meant to rise, in the quiet transcendence of a grateful soul, a soul yielded, conquered, a soul at peace with sovereignty, that it would shape itself into the very habit of our days, that worship would show its shy and lovely face in all our mirrors and in the hushed music of a surrendered life. O, that God would weep for the joy of it, for His echo's glad return. I am wild with sweetness and expectation. Let it fill the mouth where hunger feeds, the tongue by which it sings.

In Christ, my soul winged, aloft, His echo's glad return, Amen

May worship set something beautiful adrift in the chambers of the blood.

IN GOD I TRUST

In God I have put my trust…—Psalms 56:11 NKJV

*Lord, I have learned to trust so little in this world. I hold myself suspect in my abilities to manipulate life around me, to discern it accurately, to break it down to its more definable, recognizable parts. Without You I am maddened with incertitude, I am overruled by indifference and apathy, thrown helpless to the rude temper of the winds. I am only beginning to walk a path of trust. And though I cannot say with certainty that **I will** trust You in all things, for I am bound for a season to this doubtful mortality, I know **I can** trust You, that **I can** trust in Your unfailing love. In Christ, You have made me kinsman, no less Your child. May innocence be found in me to trust like that child. Set Your imprint of government upon my soul, which, like an embossed coin, may carry this oath, IN GOD I TRUST.*

In Christ, the trustworthy, my sure God, Amen

May Christ be your poverty, your riches, your coin of exchange in this world of broken men.

THEY ARE NOT LIKE US

Praise the Lord from the earth, you large sea animals and all the oceans, lightning and hail, snow and mist, and stormy winds that obey him, mountains and all hills, fruit trees and all cedars, wild animals and all cattle, crawling animals and birds…—Psalms 148:7-10 NCV

Creation itself is Your first witness, Lord. The obedient elements, the aloof and twinkling stars, all read plainly before us like an epistle of love. And You are not absent even among the beasts of the field and the lowliest of creatures. They too have a thing to say. Their instincts do not incline them to vanity, as do our own. The habits of their blood do not include ambition, promise of reward, gain for gain's sake, or the illusion of celebrity among their own kind. For these are all too human. Give me a heart that is undistracted, a mind that is free, and an eye that is worthy of both, that I may find You in places I did not suspect, that I may read the full gospel all around me. Till love refines nature in me, till love be the law in my blood.

In Christ, *the law of life sealed in the vein of every leaf, in every lift of the wind,* **Amen**

May love make you a seer, a visionary, not only to discern truth from untruth, but also to see what beauty there is in the world. For there is yet much to see that is lovely, unspoiled, creation rich. May love liberate your eyes.

LOVE AND THE PRAYER
OF THE VIGILANT

NOVEMBER 23

Watch therefore, for you do not know when the master of the house is coming—in the evening, at midnight, at the crowing of the rooster, or in the morning…—Mark 13:35 NKJV

Be vigilant, my soul. Rouse yourself. How quietly love may steal among the hours. What form will it take? What face will it assume? What voice will I recognize? How will the invitation read when it comes to me? Watch, and be instant in love! There is divinity in the smallest act of kindness. The very presence of God is summoned in the utterance of a single true and hopeful word. And you, my heart, you measure keeping, meter tapping heart, surrender hard in love's appointed time! Engage yourself fully and consider not the cost, for love and the moment will not pass this way again!

In Christ, life fully engaged, Amen

May there be a clear and unobstructed passage between your heart and your higher senses, the radar that tracks warm life around you.

For the LORD will comfort Zion, He will comfort all her waste places; He will make her wilderness like Eden, and her desert like the garden of the LORD; Joy and gladness will be found in it, Thanksgiving and the voice of melody.—Isaiah 51:3 NKJV

Thanksgiving, like worship, is not an exercise, not an event, but a way of life, a living impulse in the blood, that distills into every minor and every major detail of our lives, every inflection of our voice, every suggestion we make with our bodies, every human exchange, every exchange we make with ourselves in the secret confessional of our own mind, every act of kindness, every quiet pause, every annoyance, in all things that traffic our little worlds.

In Christ, all my gratitude, Amen

May your heart be glad at the smallest evidences of love found among the common ceremonies and rituals of your day.

A day, a Week, a Lifetime of Thanksgiving—A Prayer

NOVEMBER 25

I will praise the name of God with a song, and will magnify Him with thanksgiving.—Psalms 69:30 NKJV

Thank You, Lord, for love that remains true to itself. Thank You for loving me, not according to my own measures of love, but by remaining true to Your own. You did not indulge me nor did You allow me to fall beneath the weight of my own illusions of love. You separated me from the thing that I was and gave life to me that I had not imagined, a sweetness that is too dear and too close now for words. I live the good life. It was Your gift to me. May every day be a day of Thanksgiving. May my calendar overflow with Thursdays in November.

In Christ, *a sweetness too dear,*
all that I had not imagined, Amen

May you be numbered among the living treasures of His Heaven, the one He keeps in the protected closure of His heart. And when He looks down upon this unbright earth, may a light shine in your place. May it be beautiful in His eyes. May the thought of you be music, your very name sweet upon His lips like a song or perhaps a kiss.

EUCHARIST: THANKSGIVING

Great peace have those who love Your law, and nothing causes them to stumble.—Psalms 119:165 NKJV

All living things come to their quiet ends and all rivers flow silent beneath us until the sea. Love is constant, like the fixed and changeless God. We were maddened by it, delighted and terrified by it, and we lost our way. A gulf was fixed between heaven and ourselves and words could not mend the breach. Nor tears. There was no passage and no door. Nonetheless, a bridge was fashioned of two crude pieces of timber and a few nails. Love paid the cost and God spent Himself in the labor. *Lord, our words are nothing much in the balance of things. And what is our thanks if it be but words? Take no less than this one life. By purchase it is legally Yours. It was worth something to You. I have few rights to it. I yield what is in my power to yield. Christ has long ago settled the transaction. I trust love with the details.*

In Jesus, the bridge, the Christ of the scarlet wood, Amen

May love in you be someone's map to paradise, a well lighted path and not a labyrinth, amazing, never a maze.

A Eucharist Prayer

The cup of blessing which we bless, is it not the communion of the blood of Christ? The bread which we break, is it not the communion of the body of Christ?—1 Corinthians 10:16 NKJV

You are my deep spring, the thirst that maddens me.

You are the font where life washes itself clean of mortality.

Let me drink of Thee as lovers are bid to drink,

Let me take this liquid warrant,

This consummation, this oath in blood to my lips,

And be thankful to Him, my soul,

To that generous and life dispersing Him,

Him that reflects me, that calls back my features in the wine,

As I drink from the gilded cup,

As my mouth kisses the cool and shining rim of royal gold.

Till Him. Till essence mingles with essence.

Till God be filtered through this wasting tenement of my flesh.

ONCE IN A NIGHT OF
CANDLES AND KINGS

You number my wanderings; put my tears into Your bottle; are they not in Your book? When I cry out to You, then my enemies will turn back; this I know, because God is for me.—Psalms 56:8-9 NKJV

Last night I watched candles burning. My tears gave them limbs, liquid and starry shapes that calmly tread the brine of my watchfulness. A prayer in me was alive, laboring. The jealous and defending David wrestled from me the unkind Judas who had stolen upon me with a greeting and a kiss, putting him at last to flight and silence. My soul now at peace, I am delivered from this womb of psalms, out of this royal dark and prolific night, this generous night that had closed in so warm about me.

In Christ, in my soul like a psalm warring in my behalf, Amen

May your prayer break free of thought and invention. And of words. May the desire of God so mingle with your own, that you are no longer able to discern where humanity ends and divinity begins, by a harmony too deep for explanations, too sweet for singing.

NOVEMBER 29

The LORD God planted a garden eastward in Eden…
  —*Genesis 2:8 NKJV*

*O, for Wonder to quicken us again, to incite riots in the blood
as it did in some forgotten age past, when the earth was electric
with green, when the sky itself kept not its conversation from us,
when the stars had no riddles and told their tales like bright
twinkling gospels, when creation hid not its wisdom from our eyes.
We were not so removed and not so civilized. We were not afraid
to be ourselves. This was Eden, now a dream, now a memory in
the soul of earth, an erasure on the old maps, a thing we debate
in our Sunday Schools. O, for the time when God was not so
removed, love was not so aloof, when the cool of the day was the
coolest time. We may have little memory of it at all, for time had
no jurisdiction there, no voice or argument to raise against us.
There was only love and wet grass beneath our feet.*

In Christ, the wonder of it all, **Amen**

May love restore the innocence that made it easy to believe.

Love and Thankfulness

Give thanks to the LORD, for He is good; His love endures for ever.
—*Psalms 106:1 NIV*

Thankfulness is a perfume, worn best, as any perfume, in suggestion, not overthrow. Our life itself can be a proclamation of gratitude, not limiting our thanks to mere words or to times set aside, but in flow, steady and irrepressible, like a continuing pulse, being thankful that *LOVE IS,* thankful that *GOD IS,* for these are the high marks to which thankfulness may aspire. Not for things. Not for reward. Love is its own reward. *Love is the gratitude hidden within itself.* Heaven applauds thanksgiving that is shown in a single act of kindness. Such an act of gratitude, such a return to God on His investment in our lives, gives the angels something to sing about. *O, that I may wear it, thankfulness with so rich an essence, enchanting, inescapable, that it effuse in the air about me as I pass, not unlike the presence of God Himself. O, to be such a lover as this.*

In Christ, *such a lover as I long to be,* **Amen**

May heaviness lose itself in thanksgiving. May gladness put the springs back into the heels of life, buoyancy back into our stride.

December

Christ, our deeper nature

DECEMBER 1

...Everyone who loves is born of God and knows God.
—*1 John 4:7 NKJV*

It's that time again. Green and red will dominate our colors
and add an enchantment to life. Commerce and Christianity
will meet and labor together. The marketplace will swell with
fatness. And it's in such a world the lover is born, right in the
midst of things, in the sweep and fury of life. Perhaps even
in a shuffling, taxing time. Lovers are born in simplicity, in
lowliness, outside of money, born of dust and deity, of life and
afterlife, no less a Christ event. *Heaven said, "Now." A maiden
said, "Yes." It's how love comes into the world. It's what happens
when surrender and divinity meet.*

**In Love, what happens when surrender and divinity meet,
Amen**

May your dreams always have a Bethlehem and one bright star.

DECEMBER 2

We have thought, O God, on Your lovingkindness, in the midst of Your temple.—Psalms 48:9 NKJV

Make my soul a temple, a place where love builds its house, where the sound of singing is heard, where prayer and tenderness conspire together, where Your Word is the centerpeace. May the doors of this sacred house have no locks, no bolts. May Welcome and Benediction be written upon its beams. May it be well lighted, candled long into the night. May incense perfume its corridors, like the prayers that unsecret my soul before You. Cleanse me, O Christ. Turn over the tables of my folly and discard what I had gained by them, along with the illusions that seemed sufficient for me, the great fictions of my life that I had crafted around me, my props, my supports. Your love has unsettled me and the taste of Your sweetness, of Your spiced wine, even of this prayer still warm on my lips, I could never rid myself of.

In Christ, *my centerpeace, Amen*

May life be kind. Which kind is up to you.

I Bid You Christ!

My love be with you all in Christ Jesus. Amen.
—1 Corinthians 16:24 NKJV

I bid you Christ! Who descended our cellar depths to show us the divine within each of us, what it looked like, how it behaved, how it spoke, what tenderness felt like, what warmth could do to the soul. Love in person. *I bid you Christ!* The warlike and gentle, the dread and tender, the meek and majestic, the all human, all divine, deathless paradox of seeming opposites, Who is, ever, the just, merciful, and Almighty God.

In Christ, Love in person, Amen

May Christ be the celebration that breaks out in your soul, that invites a world to attend.

ALL OR NOTHING

DECEMBER 4

"For as the heavens are higher than the earth, So are My ways higher than your ways, and My thoughts than your thoughts."
—Isaiah 55:9 NKJV

To have any of God is to have all of Him. In the same way, if love gives of itself in the least, it gives all. It confounds our accounting perhaps, but it's love's way. Love is an all or nothing proposition. And it is complete in itself. Mountain or mustard seed, small acts, large ones, it just doesn't matter. Such measures, degrees, or comparisons don't really apply in love. They are a nonissue. Divinity and proportion are unrelatable. Dimension and magnitude are irrelevant. It just doesn't matter in love's strange economy of things. All that, to say this: *If I truly love at all, I love completely, following the whole rule of love. If I deny in the least, I deny all.*

In Christ, *the whole rule of love,* Amen

May you not fear when love assigns you to its lonely place, when the landscape about you is wild or uneven, when it is stark and empty, desolate and remote, when the light is dim and you must trust your way to the unseen God.

ALL THAT GLITTERS

They shall go into the holes of the rocks, and into the caves of the earth, from the terror of the LORD and the glory of His majesty, when He arises to shake the earth mightily.—Isaiah 2:19 NKJV

Have you ever noticed when you are in the presence of celebrity, how the awe surrounding them can be overwhelming at times? That before the mystery of greatness the heart becomes overcharged because of something unsure in us as we stand before the mythic light of fame that seems so removed from us? Considering this, what about God Himself, surrounded with mystery, with awe so thick it blinds you, with light that is alive, and with legions of angels; is it possible to be so rapt, so taken, so smitten with awe, so unsettled and distracted with all that surrounds Him, that we never really know the person at its center? *Could we mistake presence for person? Is it possible to worship that which surrounds Him and not worship Him?* It's only a question.

In Christ, the person of God, the Man within the cloak of Majesty, the light within the light, Amen

May illusion be voiceless and tame, dying among the rushes, mute, breathless. May they have no power, no jurisdiction over you. May the light of God be too efficient, too jealous.

DECEMBER 6

Bless the LORD, O my soul! O LORD my God, You are very great: You are clothed with honor and majesty…
—*Psalms 104:1 NKJV*

Turn my eyes away from gold, that I may gaze on Him alone, Christ, the God Who stood among us, Who walked upon our pavements without the gloss and trappings of the Mighty, without the pomp of earthly kings, Who trafficked among the most common of us, Who spoke in our synagogues and in our markets, Who visited our houses, ate at our tables, Who was not afraid to laugh out loud, Who wept for our lost brother, Who loved without the usual restraints, and Who would have us to love likewise, Who crowded us closely to Himself to show us the thing in His heart that was more precious than the purest and most costly treasures of the earth. Let me be not struck dumb with majesty, but worship Him Who is at the heart of it.

In Christ, love worthy of my ambitions laid down, Amen

May praise and poetry gather in your mouth and conspire together often. May they sweeten in the ear of Majesty.

CHRIST! AND BE GLAD!

Be glad and rejoice, for the LORD has done marvelous things!
—Joel 2:21 NKJV

Christ! And be glad! Lose yourself in Him! Find yourself also in Him, your world view, your theory of government, and the contentment that comes in the midst of them! *Christ! And be glad!* He is the Wondermaker, Who does Amazing so easy and with so little, Who crafts poetry from weakness, composes a hymn of life from your uncertainties, a world altering gospel from all your complications, and with things we've hidden from the world, those things in us we think of little worth, unattractive, or plain. *Christ! And be glad!* With the ink of His own wounds He wrote beauty back into the history of man. With deep groans He gave us the music to go with it.

In Jesus, the Wondermaker, our Laureate Christ, Amen

May you wake to a world that was not there when you slept last. May there be a brighter, newer sun to illumine your paths, to ennoble your hilltops. May there be something about daylight that seems kinder, more hopeful, more promising, and more forgiving than you had remembered it, even one sleep past.

ALL THAT IS WITHIN ME

DECEMBER 8

And it happened, when Elizabeth heard the greeting of Mary, that the babe leaped in her womb; and Elizabeth was filled with the Holy Spirit. —Luke 1:41 NKJV

Like you, I too am a masterwork of the odd and the beautiful, of joy and complication, a storehouse of contradictions, of contending elements that coexist beneath my surfaces, like truth and fantasy, disillusionment and faith, desperation and contentment, illusion and certitude, the sacred and the profane. I contain the meticulous record of every tender and untender moment. I contain the secrets of my unconfessed crimes, as well as too many things left untended and unrealized, things left to the rust and spoil of time. I contain greatness and smallness within the same living frame, humanity and divinity within the same crowded house. *But let all that is within me BLESS THE LORD. Let my soul leap with the joy of blessedness, the joy of one who knows Christ as kinsman and king, the joy of one awaiting his own delivery.*

In Christ, Master of this crowded house, Amen

May you know Him when He comes. May the riot and celebration that stirs in the heart be your best indicator. May love be so uncivilized in you. And so beautiful.

Stillness in the Strings

O LORD, You have searched me and known me.
—*Psalms 139:1 NKJV*

You framed the human heart for a dwelling place. You set pulses in the blood and gave a beat to life. You inquire into me. You study me with Your interrogating Spirit. Anticipation in me is quiet, like stillness in the strings that wait the touch of skill and tenderness. I know You will not leave me to my own ends, but will set my soul to order, like a song set to staves of music, with rests and stops, with bars and measures that keep time and beauty in rule together. Let this prayer be a comfort to those who find it, who share these intimate confines with me.

In Christ, my rest, my stops, my soul set to beauty, Amen

May the sacred and undeclared within you be offered up as an audible feast.

DECEMBER 10

...And I shall be whiter than snow.—*Psalms 51:7 NKJV*

It's bitter cold outside my window this morning and it seems the only thing falling from heaven is the snow. It too is quiet. Brilliant, beautiful, but silent as a shroud. The earth around me wears graveclothes of linen, soft as down. Doubt has overcome me with restraint. You who read this may think yourself fortunate not to be me today. But where is love if it hides itself, if it slips behind a curtain, if it gives nothing of itself away, and risks nothing? Where is love if it comes out but on fairer days? I will hide nothing from you here. If I break, I will gather the pieces quietly and share them with you who would not fear my silence. I am a fool perhaps, but I will give my soul the permission it needs to sing. *Save us from ourselves, O God. We are children pretending to be grown-ups. We talk love. But we do not do love. We are so civilized. And we live in shadows and disguises. Save us from this half-life.*

In Christ, my soul covered in whiteness,
a robe and not a shroud, Amen

May you allow yourself an intimate friendship with silence and may your heart learn to trust within the quiet of her shelters.

THE LAW OF LOVE

Oh, how I love Your law! It is my meditation all the day.
—*Psalms 119:97 NKJV*

No offence can alter love. Or change its mind. When there
is an offence, love transcends the offence. Love remains
love in spite of the most contrary emotions. Love does not
trust them. Love does not bargain with them. Love does
not obligate itself to them. They can be quite lawless and
inconstant. Love is parent to our child and remains true to
itself, as before a law it cannot bend. *How beautiful the law of
love! How lovely and how unquestioned! How trustworthy and how
true! Set more firm than the heavens from which it governs.*

In Christ, The Faithful, in Whom justice is content, Amen

May you love as one who loves large, as one who has lost
their hard opinion of things, whose warmth is never hoarded,
whose heart is easily broken as against a strong and sweeping
tide it cannot resist nor harness, like mercy, kindness, like
forgiveness and pardon, things that liberate the divine in each
of us and make explanation unnecessary.

WHEN THE HEART IS QUIET

DECEMBER 12

"…He will quiet you with His love, He will rejoice over you with singing."—Zephaniah 3:17 NKJV

My soul is hushed, its voice muzzled within me. The more I toil to speak the tighter the reins, the deeper and more naked the silence, still as death. I have questions with no tongue to give them shape. I have complaints with no mouth to put them in. I have praise without singing to give it flight, gratitude that has no door, no outward vent. I have jets of ebony in my veins, yet my pages are dry with thirst and silence. I cannot redeem myself with the usual charms of speech or by a lyric sweet with repentance and rhapsody. My hidden springs are but an indiscriminate murmur. I am undone. I am a vanquished city. O, my jealous God, You sought me in those places where I hid myself away. You have sealed all my escapes. As a gentle Conqueror You come over me and do violence to my distractions. You quiet me. Enter, O Lord, the gates of Your city, now silent as tombs.

In Christ, my quiet soul, this ecstasy in stillness, Amen

When the soul is emptied of itself, when the tongue lay still at last, when your petitions are exhausted, may that assurance, that warm and sheltering calm, rise with you from your prayer, may it be your quiet confidence throughout the day.

Is That Music I Hear or is Rachel Weeping?

Now I plead with you, brethren, by the name of our Lord Jesus Christ, that you all speak the same thing, and that there be no divisions among you, but that you be perfectly joined together in the same mind and in the same judgment. —1 Corinthians 1:10 NKJV

Love is bigger than belief, bigger than doctrine, bigger than our roots and our legends, bigger than our differences, bigger than the pride we celebrate in our differences. Christianity is about family, about living connectivity and genuine warmth, about love active, love present, love immediate, unreserved, unrestrained. It's about blood, uncommon blood that's common among us, blood that is stronger than our isolations. The times have told us flattering things about ourselves. It's as if some lullaby has rocked our brains and we're no longer aware how desperately we need each other, that the seams have long come undone, that we are but children, lost and scattered. *Is that music I hear or is Rachel weeping*[15]?

In Christ, Rachel's comfort, the times reinterpreted, Amen

Religion is an argument. God is love. May you begin to open your gates, pull back the heavy curtains, and unbolt the doors that were closed, that were sealed shut by the stern parent of religion, or by some imagination, some grand illusion we thought was spiritual and heavenly.

---

15 *Jeremiah 31:15, Matthew 2:18*

WARMTH AND FOREVER

DECEMBER 14

For to me, to live is Christ, and to die is gain.
  —*Philippians 1:21 NKJV*

When Warmth and Forever conceived, love became one of us.
A star was born to change the course of all our maps. And He
is no dream, no invention, no mere opiate to soothe the nerve
of humanity where it is vexed with the unexplained, no trick of
hoping man is He. *But Christ, if I live, and Christ, if I love at all.*

In Christ, Warmth and Forever in me,
registered under one name, Amen

May His sun be high enough in your skies. And may you
dare to say, "this sun is mine." The drowsy light of afternoon,
"mine." These things I cannot express, "mine." Sunset and the
dying day, the day that struggles for life in a blaze of lavenders,
golds, and shades in between, "it is mine." The strange music
that eulogizes the sun, crickets and other chirping, singing
things. A million nameless things. The dog that barks in
the muted distance, the swelling prose of a benevolent and
well-crafted darkness to whom I as much belong, and can say
"mine." Night and stillness, "mine." These vaulted heavens that
canopy my world and all the prophecies they keep, "mine."

The Treasure of All Your Maps

December 15

"I am the way, the truth, and the life."—John 14:6 NKJV

Lord, we contend as much with our future as we do with our past. We have not trusted love, for we fear the mystery of it. We fear the uncertain way. And yet the illusions we trusted in are empty and have left us wanting. We fed on air. We sought phantoms. We took shadows as being real. We sought the dream of love and not love itself, for love was much too powerful, too high for us in our misadventures. Be merciful to me in my ignorance and in my unsatisfaction, for I have yet to believe so doubtless, to trust so deep, to hope so long as you have desired of me. I am haunted by the ghost of my truest self. Lead me. I will trust my care to You and to the love that may banish them.

In Christ, my banished care, my soul untroubled, Amen

May Christ be the treasure of all your maps, where all desire in you leads, where the soul may shepherd itself to richness.

WHERE THE COALS BLUSH

DECEMBER 16

But if I say, "I will not mention him or speak any more in his name," his word is in my heart like a fire, a fire shut up in my bones. I am weary of holding it in; indeed, I cannot.
—*Jeremiah 20:9 NIV*

Entrust Your desire to me, Lord. Draw back the curtain where You dream, where longing in You hides itself, that I may show myself loyal to that which moves Your heart, a good steward to the deep craving in You, that I may give myself completely to what pleases You, till contentment warms in Your breast. May Your unrest be my unrest, Your delight my delight. And I know that I am as much a part of Your desire, that I am as much the subject of Your inwardness. So gather my soul to that hearth where the secret fire glows, where the coals blush with delight. And there let me abide.

Warm and in love, **Amen**

May you live in some form of wondrous overwhelm.

A Dispute Among Gods

"No one can serve two masters; for either he will hate the one and love the other, or else he will be loyal to the one and despise the other. You cannot serve God and mammon."
—*Matthew 6:24 NKJV*

Money is perhaps the visible god of this earth. We express awe. We assign mystery to it, as well as majesty, preeminence. We revere the one with much of it. We pursue it. We're maddened by it. We follow its laws and commands. We obey its prophets and teachers. We seek them out. They are the oracles of our time. We are happy in abundance of it. We despair in low tide. Our emotions are effected by it. We ache in the absence of it. Do I have to go on? *The issue is* **Who do you serve?** *There can be but one God. And remember: the name JUDAS means 'praise.'*

In Christ, where the dispute ends, Amen

Christ! And be glad! May He stand high and counter to all the lesser, more visible gods of this world: money, ambition, power, influence, fashion. May He be your lucid God, your clarity in all things.

At the Foot of the Mountain

Now Mount Sinai was completely in smoke, because the LORD descended upon it in fire. Its smoke ascended like the smoke of a furnace, and the whole mountain quaked greatly.
—*Exodus 19:18 NKJV*

Lord, we stood and gazed at the foot of the mountain, the mountain of Your Presence covered in darkness and smoke, that quaked with thunder, that burned with hidden and unquenchable fire, whose mystery terrified us. You tarried and we began to dance around the idols we had made. We sang and maddened ourselves with wine. We fed our passions and called it love. Save us from our blindness. Let the earth shake beneath us once again Lord! Let surrender and obedience, awe and silence rise up in our camps. Open up the deep springs and let Your waters wash over us and cleanse us from ourselves. Let love be satisfied in us. For You are my life's debt, O Christ. You are my shield, my refuge, my shelter at the first hint of thunder.

In Christ, the hidden and unquenchable fire in me, Amen

May God Himself, the good Father, watch over you and come for you in the hour you call, moving heaven and earth and all the elements to save you from the fear of one troubling moment.

THE ONLY THING THAT COUNTS!

The only thing that counts is faith expressing itself through love.
  —Galatians 5:6 NIV

Out of which starting gate have you ever seen race horses
amble and lope till they felt better about themselves or till
it was explained to them more thoroughly what all the fuss
was about before they bolted to the finish line? Nope! It was
one good kick, then instinct, genetics, training, and something
wild in them loose for just a brief turn to call down thunder
upon the tracks. *The gate is open! The alarm is ringing! The pitch
is high! The blood is up! You have all the permissions you need!
You've studied the manual! You have your command! You can do
this! Just love people! It's the only thing that counts! Summon up
all your faith! Put your Christianity to it's finest paces! And just
love people! Love! And be joyful! Christ! And be glad!*

In Christ, the day that waits before you like a prize, Amen

May you be so absorbed in love, so profoundly smitten, so
continuously raptured, so gloriously illuminated by love's all
consuming brightness, that all lesser things pale, that faith
itself is caught up, consumed, even as the sun steals the moon
from our sight and chases away the last stars of morning.

WHO WOKE THE UNIVERSE
IN SPLENDOR

DECEMBER 20

For You will light my lamp; the LORD my God will enlighten my darkness.—Psalms 18:28 NKJV

I have lived in blindness and twilight for too long. I am weary with distrust, distrust of what I have become and what I know. Therefore, dash my perceptions upon the rocks, grind them to dust and insignificance by the rude traffic of a million inconveniences if You must. And though I howl like an ungrateful child, ransom my eyes. Come like Wonder and Daybreak over me O Founding Dawn, O First Light, Primalspeak of God, Who woke the universe in Splendor, gave it Majesty and Brilliance and all at the utterance of a Word! Let light be!

In Christ, Who woke the universe in Splendor, Amen

When the universe was given eyes to see at last, Christ was the light that made it possible. May He be your sight, your blindness, your bright and deathless candle.

ROMANCE: A DEEPER NATURE

Love has been perfected among us in this: that we may have boldness in the day of judgment; because as He is, so are we in this world.
—1 John 4:17 NKJV

In the early stages of romance, reason is banished. Rule is overthrown. There is only anarchy. I can look back on my own experience and think, *'How did she and I survive our beginnings?'* Or even as a new believer, *'How did I keep from poisoning myself with excess?'* To this day I have no answer. I suspect love. Like a conqueror of cities, love established its own law, its own divine order that reordered us. So what happens to the boy when she gives him the wonder of her YES, that delicious, unsettling and world overthrowing YES? He *thinks* he's a god. And maybe he's not so far from wrong, that in his innocence, in this newly awakened riot of joy, he has rediscovered something, as a thing lost to him in a forgotten age, refound in the primordial sediments of the memory, loosed in love.

In Christ, *our deeper nature, Amen*

May love teach you the way of intimacy, its surrenders, its glorious martyrdoms, its anticipations, its regulation of the pulse. May you be a good student and may you develop instincts that, like the love of Christ, are beyond human likeness.

ALL IS EDEN, BUT NOT YET PARADISE

DECEMBER 22

"It is not good that man should be alone…"—*Genesis 2:18 NKJV*

Everything is new. The garden is green and alive with things that he named himself. The eager synapses of his brain are running on overwhelm. And questions, endless questions. After all, who has been here before to tell of these things? He is the first of his strange kind. There are no others. *All is Eden, but not yet Paradise.* The newness fades and it is then he begins to notice. Not knowing what it is to feel pain and want, he detects a new, puzzling, and yet not totally unpleasant sensation in his side. He is haunted by the presence of a thing he knows is not divine and yet is too fine and too lovely in his thoughts to be earthly. It is so close to him and yet the planets and the newly lighted stars above him seem closer and more merciful. Paradise was in him from the beginning. Then he awoke.

**In Christ, *too fine and too lovely to be of
this earth alone,* Amen**

May that which is unborn in you have the seal of divinity upon it and may love lead you to the Bethlehem that will bring it forth, that will introduce it to the world.

A NATIVITY PRAYER

Dear friends, we should love each other, because love comes from God.
—1 John 4:7 NCV

This season can be overpowering, Lord. Sweetness and antiquity have come together again to celebrate something old and beautiful in the blood. Let us not be lost in our distractions. Let us celebrate our true nativity. Let us remember the pain that labored us here, that made us children of the Most High, Love that imposed itself upon a young maiden, love that grew in her till she cried out in a night that gave Christ to the world. O, let heaven rest in me, even as it did on that cradled and quiet night so long ago, when her prince was given to us.

In Jesus, my true nativity, Amen

May the *wise man* in you find his star. May it sparkle in your skies like a bright jewel you cannot ignore or lose in your distractions. May it lead you to the Bethlehem of your latter nativity, the womb of life that will offer you to an ungospelled world, that will set another lover, another lamb adrift in a world of the loveless and unsure.

December 24

For behold, henceforth all generations will call me blessed. For He who is mighty has done great things for me, and holy is His name.
—*Luke 1:46-49 NKJV*

She was the first to know, the first to hear from angels' lips the gospel of His coming. The first to hold Him. The first to feel His hunger. The first to know the gentle rhythms of His heart. When love sought a door, a passage of entry, a mother to child itself into this world, she offered up her will, her consent, her body. And Christianity had its first stirrings, cradled sweet in the surrender and in the womb of a maiden.

In Jesus, the son of Mary and the Christ within her, Amen

May you enjoy all the blessings that have been assigned to you, as well as some you never would have expected, for heaven is full of surprises when it mingles with things of earth and faithfulness.

Christmas Day: The Day That Gave Me the Right to Say I'm in Love

"For unto us a Child is born, Unto us a Son is given;

And the government will be upon His shoulder.

And His name will be called Wonderful, Counselor,

Mighty God, Everlasting Father, Prince of Peace."

—Isaiah 9:6 NKJV

May love overflow your tables, in warm unceasing measures of Him Who is our feast, Jesus, our one and lovely Christ of all seasons.

THE DAY AFTER

DECEMBER 26

"…I am with you always, even to the end of the age." Amen.
— *Matthew 28:20 NKJV*

It is the day after. The deflation now begins, a slow leak
in the mirth and the forgetfulness of the season but a few
hours past. The hopeful greens, the warm reds, the goblet
golds, and the trumpeting silvers, all will slowly fade to steel
winter gray. The music, as quickly as it came to us, as quickly
passes. *When from the fallout of a single day, when all mystery
is unwrapped and all strings undone, when wild joy is old and
tame, when feasting ends and the charm winds down, when we
have come to ourselves again, Lord, Your love is, After All.*

In Christ, After All, Christ, in the too quiet hour, Amen

May love distill into all of your life, to the very particulars.
May it bestow divinity to the most common elements of
it, that on the dullest of days love may raise its beams and
columns of light and warmth about you, a cathedral, a
temple, a house of peace.

THE DAY AFTER THE DAY AFTER

"Glory to God in the highest, and on earth peace, goodwill toward men!"—Luke 2:14 NKJV

Lord, redeem us in this declining time. Exhausted, spent, the bright season begins to steal slowly away and with its own mysterious burden on its back, taking from us perhaps as much as it brought. The spell is over. Call quiet upon us. Gather us to Yourself before winter blasts in our faces, before we burrow beneath our surfaces, before Lonely has a chance to brood among us once again. Let Your assurances preserve us. Let love warm us ever and deep within its soft down coverings. Companion those neglected and overlooked. Shelter the homeless and unprotected. Let blessedness rule among us. Be gladness to us, Lord, our unending festival. For long after our revels end, You Are. Keep me.

In Christ, *the day after the day after and then some,* **Amen**

May anticipation of Him give the day back its color. May it bring pinkness to the cheeks, celebration to the heart, and thanksgiving to the tongue.

CHRIST, THE SHAPE OF
THINGS TO COME

DECEMBER 28

Whom have I in heaven but You? And there is none upon earth that I desire besides You.—Psalms 73:25 NKJV

Christ is the deep request of every heart in all lives that people this distracted planet. For all were made in love, for love, and by a God Who is love. Christ is not some aloof or separate event in the chronicle of man. He is the necessary event. Christ, the inevitable, the watermark, the deep imprint of God upon the soul of Everyman. In each of us there is an emptiness a hollowness only love can fill and Christ is the shape it takes, for love can be but one thing, as God can be but one thing It's a part of our nature too deep, yet too misunderstood. Jonah still crying out in the abyss of mankind, Eden still being sought among us.

In Christ, the shape of things to come, Amen

May you not despair in what seems to be no response, or at best, a slow response from God. When you cry out to Him, the crying out itself is its own fulfillment, for God hides Himself in your very hunger for Him. *It's Him we want. To call out to Him is to have Him in the same instant. The pain is the cure. Another riddle of love.*

THE MEMORY OF ME

For with You is the fountain of life; In Your light we see light.
  —*Psalms 36:9 NKJV*

O, Bright God, make me invisible, as light that loses itself in a greater light, till You alone be seen in me, till love shine through all my surfaces. Love, more jealous, that rages more violent than fire, love, larger than this one life, love, with a greater sovereignty than death. Love, inescapable, like this arc of sky above me or the coming night that shelters me beneath its dark wing, love, that rises like daybreak upon this sleeping world, that gives to each new morning a hope, a possibility, an overmastering and deified YES. O God, haunt me with favor! Fret me with Your goodness till I ache with joy, till I weep under the blessed penalty of it! Busy me with delight, intolerable and fair, till love be enthroned in me, immovable, imperial, till love gets the better of me, till You be revealed through this sheer curtain of me, till I be gone at last, till I am nothing more than a memory to myself.

In Christ, the memory of me, Amen

May the unsuspecting world marvel at what they can easily see inside you and by a brave and brilliant light that is all yours.

December 30

For all the law is fulfilled in one word, even in this: "You shall love your neighbor as yourself."—*Galatians 5:14 NKJV*

I have dared to open my mouth and spend all my idiot commentary and on one subject, love. I come to the table every day either with my engines humming or I am blank, full of myself, drowsy, or grumbling, but nonetheless it's daily, with my thoughts fixed on one thing, love. And how fortunate! How sweet it is to rise! How unlike my former days. I'm being transformed and I'm terrified. But that's not a bad thing. Perhaps it's a necessary thing. It actually liberates me. Yes, I am afraid. Not in the doing of the task, but more and more in the subject for which I task myself. I just did not know the magnitude of it. I had taken love so lightly, so casually, depending on my own assessments. Now I am awake and can never see the same again. O, what a God! And I wonder why I ever thought or spoke of anything else. I am smitten. Love does that.

In Christ, *if love speaks at all, Amen*

May a healer rise up from within you, walk in your footsteps, speak with your voice, and warm the earth with tenderness.

LOVE AND AT THE LAST DAY

"I am the Alpha and the Omega, the Beginning and the End, the First and the Last."—Revelation 22:13 NKJV

Is there no warm eulogy to comfort us at the passing of this year? What epitaph newly written will answer for that which is behind me now, Time, whose least division cannot be called back again? Did love write a new testimony on the heart? And did it labor in stone? What moments, what calendar marks, as I look back, can report *"Something wonderful happened here!"* or *"Love had a moment of triumph here!"* O, that I may simply say I loved. That such a brief eulogy would be all the tribute necessary. That love had a chance in this world. That I may say that love had government in me, that there was little resistance to love's charge over me, that I yielded to its least request of me. O, that I may say that love found a friend, a kinsman in me, one of its own. That I may say I am no longer the thing I was, that the life I knew is but a history, a memory, a year and another death behind me now.

In Christ, *another death closer to home, Amen*

May you redeem the time, remembering that eternity within you is its master, that nothing is lost in love's economy.

DAVID TEEMS

This book, which is David's first, was over two years in the making and, like most memorable books, was sifted from the general busyness of living, in the midst of things, at the quick of life. David received a BA in Psychology from Georgia State University and was in graduate school when music and the distractions of youth called him away. In time he heard another call, a larger, deeper, more permanent one, that not only brought him back to the faith he had accepted as a child and had abandoned in college, but also to print. David Teems and his wife, Benita, live in Franklin, Tennessee, near their two sons, Shad, a college student, and Adam and his wife, Katie. More at *davidteems.com*.